Harmoni-Us Marriage

Elevate Your Marriage With Self-Awareness

A Practical guide for a Healthy Marriage by a Relationship Coach

AJIT KUMAR
Relationship Coach, Certified Mediator and Family Lawyer

LEGAL MIND

Books-New Delhi

To Contact Ajit Kumar for speaking arrangements and coaching, please email legalmindajitkumar@gmail.com

SELF-HELP/INSPIRATIONAL

Published in India by Legal Mind.

ISBN : 978-81-924969-1-7
□ 350/- (e-book)

Table of Contents

INTRODUCTION

In the present realities of life, where relationships and connections are essential but unpredictable, have you ever wondered why some marriages flourish while others battle to survive? The key to an effective and successful marriage isn't written in the stars but found within ourselves. Welcome to *Harmoni-Us Marriage: Elevate Your Marriage With Self-Awareness*, a transformative journey with self exploration into the foundation of marital success.

Marriage, frequently viewed as the cornerstone of society, is a excursion that begins long before vows are exchanged. It starts with self-awareness—an essential yet often ignored element, which is foundation for building a strong, satisfying and fulfilling relationship. In today's fast-paced world, external pressures, cultural differences/assumptions and societal expectations frequently overshadow personal growth, making self-awareness an essential ingredient in keeping a solid marriage.

This book dives into the multifaceted intricacies of human connection, uncovering how past experiences, attachment styles, and capacity to understand people on a deeper level (Emotional Intelligence) shape marital dynamics. It challenges the common misconception that a successful marriage is based solely upon understanding and obliging one's partner. Instead, it emphasizes that true marital harmony starts with a profound understanding of oneself.

What sets *Harmoni-Us: Elevate Your Marriage with Self-Awareness* apart is its unique approach to relationship health and wellness. Rather than offering handy solutions or one-size-fits-all arrangements, this book guides readers on an inward journey of self-discovery to bring a transformation. By blending ancient wisdom with modern psychological knowledge, it gives a comprehensive and holistic approach for nurturing a flourishing marital relationship. From time-honored ancient Indian practices like meditation and mindfulness to Modern world principles of emotional intelligence to understand individual on a deeper level and attachment theory, this book overcomes any barrier by bridging the gap between traditional and modern perspectives on relationship wellbeing.

At its basic core, *Harmoni-Us Marriage* explores five key parts crucial for achieving marital success:

1. **Self-Awareness** – The foundation of any sound and satisfying relationship. Understanding personal values, needs, and boundaries is essential before forming a meaningful connection with a partner. This book provides practical exercises to assist readers to liberate from subconscious patterns that influence their relationships and make safe and satisfying relationship.

2. **Attachment Styles & Relationship Patterns** – Drawing from attachment theory, the book investigates how early experiences shape assumptions, create expectations and form behaviors in adult relationships. By recognizing these patterns, readers can break free

from undesirable cycles and create more secure and satisfying connections.

3. **Emotional Intelligence & Self-Regulation** – Managing emotions and feelings effectively is key to maintaining marital harmony. This book not only explains emotional intelligence but also offers pragmatic approach and activities for developing emotional resilience and conflict resolution skills.

4. **Overcoming Limiting Beliefs & Self-Sabotage or Destructive Behaviour**– Many people carry subconscious convictions about relationships that come from past experiences or cultural molding. These beliefs can prompt behaving in destructive ways that obstruct in marital happiness. *Harmoni-Us Marriage* helps readers identify, challenge, and replace these restricting beliefs with enabling ones.

5. **Self-Love & Confidence** – A healthy relationship begins with a strong sense of self-worth and self-identity. By practicing self-care, self-validation, and confidence-building techniques, readers will cultivate the inner strength necessary for a flourishing relationship.

Harmoni-Us Marriage is written for anyone looking to work on and improves their relationship—whether love birds, newlyweds, long-term partners, or any singles planning for future responsibilities. It is particularly important for people who feel trapped in recurring relationship patterns, struggle with communication and emotional regulation, or wish to extend their connection with their partner. In a world where divorce rates are high and relationship satisfaction often declines over time, this book offers a roadmap for lasting change and sense of fulfillment.

Reading this book is more than just gaining information—it is embarking on a journey of personal transformation for a healthy marriage. Readers will develop a deeper understanding of themselves, acquire practical skills for emotional regulation and communication, and learn to identify attachment styles and overcome limiting beliefs that may be holding them back from true intimacy. Most importantly, they will discover how to cultivate self-love, self-identity and confidence—the foundation of all healthy relationships.

The insights and strategies shared in this book are not mere theoretical concepts; they are actionable tools that can be applied immediately to enhance relationships. Each chapter is accompanied by exercises and reflections, allowing readers to personalize their learning experience. Whether through meditation practices, attachment style evaluations, or directed journaling prompts, readers will actively engage with the material and implement meaningful changes in their lives.

One of the most powerful aspects of *Harmoni-Us Marriage* is in its emphasis on personal responsibility. While external factors and partners can impact a relationship, enduring and lasting change begins inside.

This book encourages readers to assume responsibilities for their personal growth and happiness, prompting a positive and expanding effect in their marriage. This shift in perspective can be liberating, opening up additional possibilities for connection and closeness.

Moreover, the book recognizes that any transformation requires some investment of time. Developing self-awareness and changing deep rooted patterns is a cycle that requires patience and commitment to the process. To support this journey, *Harmoni-Us Marriage* presents a structured approach, breaking down complex ideas into digestible learning lessons. Each chapter builds upon the last one, permitting readers to develop their understanding and execute changes at a comfortable pace.

While the essential spotlight is on self-awareness and self-improvement with personal growth mindset, *Harmoni-Us Marriage* also highlights how individual transformation enhances the marital dynamic. As readers become more self-aware and emotionally intelligent, they normally become better partners—more fit for understanding and addressing their life partner's needs and necessities.

This book likewise addresses common marital challenges, such as communication impasse, issues related to trust deficit, and conflict resolution, but from a personalized perspective. Instead of offering conventional advice, it helps readers understand how their individual attachment style and beliefs contribute to these challenges, making solutions more successful and sustainable.

One of the greatest strengths of *Harmoni-Us Marriage* is its encompassing approach to relationships. It recognizes that marriages don't exist in isolation but are affected by personal narratives, family dynamics, cultural assumptions and societal expectations. By addressing these various layers, the book gives a comprehensive framework for understanding and developing relationships.

The author's methodology is both compassionate and challenging. While perceiving the difficulties that many couples face, the book keeps an optimistic tone, emphasizing that change is conceivable with the right mindset and tools. It encourages readers to step out of their comfort zones, face uncomfortable truths, and take proactive steps toward a positive growth. This harmony of support and challenge establishes an environment conducive to true transformation.

Furthermore, *Harmoni-Us Marriage* integrates diverse and more often than not contradictory perspectives. While rooted in psychological research, it also draws from ancient Indian wisdom like Meditation and Pranayama, acknowledging that different cultures and philosophies offer valuable insights into relationships. This inclusive approach makes the book relevant to a broad spectrum of audience, transcending cultural and geographical boundaries.

As readers progress through the book, they will find that each chapter builds upon the last, creating a comprehensive understanding of self and relationships. For example, the self-awareness developed in the first chapter established the groundwork for understanding attachment styles in the second. The ability to understand people on deeper level by emotional intelligence cultivated in the third chapter supports the process of overcoming self-limiting beliefs in the fourth. All these elements meet up in the final chapter, which centers around building self-love and confidence.

One of the most engaging aspects of this book is how it redefines the idea of a "successful" marriage. Instead of measuring success by longevity or the absence of conflict, it stresses the nature and quality of connection, self-awareness for personal and relation growth, and shared help. It urges readers to view marriage as a vehicle for individual and shared growth—a perspective that can reinvigorate even the most settled relationships.

The exercises throughout the book are designed to be both challenging and fulfilling. They range from straightforward self-reflection inquiries to more profound practices such as meditation, pranayama and journaling. These exercises fill different needs: reinforcing key ideas, working with self-discovery, and providing substantial ways of carrying out change in real life.

Although grounded in psychological principles, *Harmoni-Us Marriage* is written in an accessible, engaging style that makes complex concepts of human psychology easy to understand. The author uses relatable examples and incidents to illustrate key points, ensuring that the material resounds with readers' regular experiences.

As you turn the last page of this introduction, you stand at the brink of an extraordinary and transformative journey. The insights and tools in the following chapters have the potential to not only improve your marriage but fundamentally transform and bringing a shift how you see yourself and your relationships. Whether you seek to resolve conflicts, develop your connection, or basically grow as an individual and a partner in relationship, *Harmoni-Us Marriage* provides the direction you need.

Are you ready to embark on this journey of self-disclosure and self-transformation further transforming your relationship? The way to a more satisfying marriage begins with the first solitary step—understanding yourself before you understand others. As you push through the chapters forward, remember that each insight acquired and each exercise completed brings you closer to the relationship you desire. Your journey to a more consciously connected, and satisfying marriage starts now.

Part 1: Understanding Yourself Before Understanding Others

Chapters:

1. Importance of self-awareness in relationships
2. How past experiences shape relationship patterns
3. Identifying personal values, needs, and boundaries
4. Achieve Self-awareness by Meditation & Pranayama

Chapter 1

Importance of self-awareness in relationships

Self-awareness plays an important role in maintaining a strong and enjoyable relationship. It means understanding your thoughts, emotions, and behaviors and recognizing how they affect your spouse in marriage. When individuals evolve with their self-awareness, they are likely to communicate better, handle disagreements with maturity, which deepens their emotional connection with their spouse.

Self-awareness entails, the below three key abilities:

- Recognizing and understanding your emotions.
- Applying your emotions to resolve relationship challenges.
- Regulating your emotions adequately.

Once you can manage your own emotions, you can begin to recognize and empathize your partner's emotions and perceptions. This awareness makes it easier to appreciate with and respond to your partner in ways that strengthen your relationship

1. Identifying and understanding your Emotional Triggers

Everyone has emotional triggers shaped by past experiences or upbringing. These triggers often stem from past experiences, childhood upbringing, or personal insecurities. These triggers can influence reactions in relationships. For instance, if Rahul was raised in a home where emotions were rarely discussed, he may find it difficult to express affection toward his wife, Priya. By becoming self-aware of this, he can make a conscious effort to show love in ways that Priya values. This Recognizing and managing emotional triggers through self-awareness can lead to better understanding and fewer unnecessary conflicts.

2. Enhancing Communication

Self-awareness enhances communication by allowing individuals to express their thoughts and feelings honestly, clearly and respectfully. For example, after a tiring day, Meera might feel irritated and unknowingly snap at her husband, Arjun. Without being self-awareness, it could lead to tension. A self-aware individual would acknowledge her stress and communicate it, saying something like, "I had a rough day and need a little time to relax before we talk." This can prevent misunderstandings and create a more conducive environment at home. This leads to more open and healthy dialogues, strengthening the emotional bond between partners.

3. Setting Realistic Expectations

Expectations play a big role in relationships, and unreasonable ones often lead to frustration and misunderstanding in relationship leading to trust issues. Self-awareness helps individuals understand their needs realistically and communicate them effectively. For instance, Ramesh might expect grand romantic gestures, while Ananya prefers expressing love through daily actions of fulfilling needs and care. If they are unaware of these differences through self-awareness, frustration can build up. Recognizing and discussing different ways of expressing love helps create balance and mutual appreciation.

4. Handling Conflicts Maturely

Disagreements are a natural part of relationships, but self-awarencss can help resolve them constructively. When partners acknowledge their own shortcomings, they are more likely to work towards solutions rather than blame each other. For example, if a couple argue over household chores, a Self-aware partner might recognize their habit to procrastinate and acknowledge it, instead of becoming defensive and accusing their spouse of nagging. This acknowledgement through self-awareness and work on improving, leads to a healthier and more cooperative dynamic and any escalation into long-term resentment.

5. Strengthening Emotional Bonds

Trust and understanding form the foundation of emotional closeness. When individuals are in touch with their feelings, they can share them more openly with their partner. Consider Ravi and Sunita, a couple married for decades who still take time to share their thoughts and experiences. Their strong emotional connection is a result of continuous, honest conversations. By practicing self-awareness, partners can create a safe space for open communication and emotional support.

6. Encouraging Personal Growth

A thriving relationship consists of two individuals who continuously learn and grow. Self-awareness highlights areas that need improvement and helps individuals take positive action. For example, if Sneha realizes she avoids difficult conversations, she can improve upon to become more open, clear and assertive in expressing her feelings and needs. When both partners focus on self-improvement, they strengthen their relationship, making it more fulfilling and resilient.

Conclusion

Self-awareness is the foundation and a powerful tool in building a strong and trustful relationship. By understanding oneself, managing emotions, and communicating effectively, couples can foster a much profound bond and create a more supportive and loving partnership. Developing self-awareness is a continuous and evolving process, but its impact on a relationship is invaluable. When individuals make an effort to grow and reflect, they set the stage for a meaningful and long lasting connection. As the saying goes, *"If you want to bring change in your surroundings, first bring a change in yourself"*.

Chapter 2

How Past Experiences Shape Relationship Patterns

Our past plays a major role in shaping how we think, feel, and behave in relationships. Whether we realize it or not, our experiences from childhood and past relationships influence the way we interact with our partners today. Understanding these influences through self-aware approach can help us build a stronger, healthier marriage.

The Impact of Early Relationships

From a young age, we learn about love, trust, and emotional security from our caregivers. If we grow up in a supportive and affectionate home, we are more likely to form secure relationships as adults. However, if we experience neglect, frequent conflicts, or emotional distance, we may unknowingly carry those patterns into our own relationships.

Take Priya, for example. She grew up in a household where her parents frequently argued but never resolved their conflicts. As a result, she developed a fear of confrontation. Whenever she and her husband, Arjun, had a disagreement, she either shut down or became defensive. It wasn't until she recognized this pattern that she consciously worked on improving her communication skills. Over time, she learned to express her feelings calmly and listen to Arjun without fear.

Understanding attachment styles can also provide insight into these patterns. People with a secure attachment style generally build trusting relationships, while those with anxious or avoidant attachment styles may struggle with closeness or fear of abandonment. Becoming aware of these tendencies helps in making healthier choices in relationships.

Learning from Past Relationships

Previous relationships including childhood experiences leave a deep impact on our emotions. If we have faced betrayal, heartbreak, or emotional neglect, we may unknowingly carry those wounds into our marriage. This can lead to trust issues, emotional barriers, or recurring conflicts.

For instance, Raj had been in a past relationship where he was often criticized, making him feel like he was never good enough. When he married Aisha, he would become overly defensive whenever she gave him feedback. He assumed she was judging him, just like his ex had. However, once Raj became self-aware and realized that Aisha's words came from love rather than criticism, he was able to respond with openness rather than fear.

Self-awareness helps us in self evaluation by understanding our own emotions and nature of attachment is the starting point before understanding of emotional trigger points or moment and situation, which guides to break free from unhealthy patterns. When we reflect on past experiences and acknowledge their impact, we can make conscious choices to respond differently. Instead of reacting from pain, we can build relationships based on trust and understanding.

Breaking Negative Cycles

Many couples face recurring issues without understanding why. Conflicts may escalate in the same way every time, or one partner may withdraw emotionally out of fear. Recognizing these patterns is the first step toward change.

Steps to Break Free:

1. **Identify and Recognize Triggers** – Notice when you react strongly to something your partner says or does. Triggers are the sparks that ignite emotional reactions. For example, a critical remark from a colleague might trigger feelings of inadequacy. By identifying such triggers, you can prepare yourself to respond calmly. Notice the physical sensations—shortness of breath, a racing heart,

or tightness in your chest. These signals are your body's way of alerting you to an emotional response. Are you responding to the present situation, or is it linked to an old wound?

2. **Challenge Negative Beliefs** – If past experiences have led you to believe that love is conditional or trust is fragile, question these beliefs. These pre-conceived notions may be false perceptions generated due to your own past experiences, which might not be correct in your current situation. Try to analyze, do they reflect your current reality?

3. **Communicate Honestly** – Share your past experiences and fears with your partner. Openness allows you to communicate better and creates an atmosphere for deeper understanding and emotional safety.

4. **Seek Guidance** – Talking to a therapist or counselor can help uncover deep-rooted patterns and guide you toward healing.

5. **Practice Self-Reflection** – Journaling, meditation, or simply taking quiet moments to reflect on your emotions can help build emotional awareness and resilience.

While our past influences us, it need not have to define us. Marriage offers a chance to create new, healthy patterns based on mutual understanding and growth.

Consider this example, Anjali and Rohan, who both came from families with a history of unhappy marriages. Fearing that their relationship would end in the same way, they made a conscious decision to break the cycle. They attended marriage counseling, read books on healthy relationships, and practiced open communication. Over time, they built a marriage based not on past fears, but on the love and respect they nurtured together.

By developing self-awareness, we take control of our relationships rather than letting past experiences control us. Instead of being shaped by old wounds or false notions, we can become the authors of our own love story—one that is healthy, fulfilling, and built on a strong foundation of trust and emotional connection.

Chapter 3

Understanding Your Personal Values, Needs, and Boundaries

Marriage is a lifelong journey that flourishes with understanding, open communication, and mutual respect. A key aspect of maintaining a strong and happy relationship is knowing your personal values, recognizing your needs, and setting healthy boundaries. These elements shape your expectations, interactions, and overall satisfaction in your marriage. Without self-awareness, misunderstandings, frustration, and unmet emotional needs can create tension between partners.

Understanding Personal Values

Values are the core beliefs that guide our decisions and priorities. They influence how we approach relationships and determine what we seek in a marriage. Common values include honesty, loyalty, family, career growth, spirituality, and financial stability.

To identify your core values, ask yourself:

- What are the three most important principles that guide my life?
- How do these values influence my expectations in marriage?

- Do my spouse and I share similar values, or are there conflicts?

For example, Priya values family time and emotional connection, while her husband, Rohan, prioritizes career growth. Understanding and respecting each other's values can help them find a balance that works for both.

Recognizing Personal Needs

Needs in a marriage go beyond daily necessities; they include emotional, psychological, and relational needs. While some needs are universal—such as love, respect, and appreciation—others are personal and unique to each individual. A partner having deep rooted value of keeping "self identity" may prioritize his/her need seeking self identity through a legitimate expectation from partner by involving in minor/major decisions in the relationship.

To understand your personal needs, reflect on:

- Do I feel loved through words of affirmation, physical affection, or acts of service?
- What kind of emotional support do I need from my partner during stressful times?
- Do my intellectual and social needs feel fulfilled in this relationship?

For instance, Meera needs verbal reassurance and quality time to feel secure in her marriage, while her husband, Arjun, expresses love through actions rather than words. By openly communicating their needs, they can strengthen their bond.

Establishing Healthy Boundaries

Healthy relationships thrive on setting clear boundaries. Boundaries define what is acceptable and unacceptable in a relationship. These might include personal space, privacy, or time for self-reflection/Me-time. They help maintain emotional well-being, encourage mutual respect, and prevent unnecessary conflicts. Boundaries can be physical, emotional, or psychological.

Examples of healthy boundaries in marriage include:

- Letting your partner know when you need alone time or personal space.
- Setting limits on work, extended family, or friendships to prioritize your marriage.
- Respecting each other's emotions without judgment or criticism.

For example, Raj works long hours and needs quiet time to unwind, while his wife, Sita, enjoys discussing her day in detail. By setting a boundary—such as giving Raj 30 minutes of alone time before their evening conversations—they create a balance that works for both.

Aligning Values, Needs, and Boundaries in Your Marriage

When couples openly discuss their values, needs, and boundaries, they can prevent conflicts and deepen their connection. Here are some practical steps to achieve this:

1. **Open Communication:** Regularly talk about what matters to you and listen to your partner's perspective.

2. **Compromise and Flexibility:** Identify your non-negotiable needs and calmly communicate them without judgment and hostility. Differences will arise, but finding common ground ensures both partners feel valued.

3. **Periodic Reassessment:** As life evolves, so do personal values and needs. Reevaluate and adjust accordingly to maintain a fulfilling relationship.

Conclusion

A marriage built on self-awareness and open communication fosters emotional security, deep connection, and long-term happiness. By understanding and respecting your personal values, needs, and boundaries, you create a relationship based on authenticity, trust, and mutual respect. As you grow individually, your marriage strengthens, evolving into a partnership filled with love and emotional balance.

Chapter 4

Achieve Self-Awareness by Meditation and Pranayama

A flourishing marriage is built on the foundation of self-awareness. Without understanding ourselves—our thoughts, emotions, feelings and responses—we might struggle to communicate our feelings effectively and build a meaningful connection with our partner. One of the best ways of developing self-awareness is through meditation and pranayama (breath control). These ancient Indian practices not only calm the mind but also help us acquiring deeper understanding into our emotions, feelings, thoughts, and behavioral patterns, which, in turn, can significantly enhance our marital relationship.

The Role of Meditation in Self-Awareness

Meditation is a useful and powerful tool that brings us into the moment to moment awareness, helping us closely observe our thoughts without judgment. When we meditate regularly, we develop the ability to pause before reacting (contemplate), allowing us to respond to our partner with greater persistence and understanding.

Benefits of Meditation in Marriage

1. **Improves Emotional Regulation:** By meditating daily, we develop emotional resilience, reducing the possibilities of impulsive reactions and unnecessary arguments.

2. **Enhances Empathy and Compassion:** Meditation fosters a sense of connectedness, empowering us to understand and empathize with our partner's emotions.

3. **Reduces Stress and Anxiety:** A calm mind allows us to approach relationship challenges with clarity and rationality.

4. **Increases Self-Reflection:** Meditation helps us become aware of our own patterns and triggers, making it easier to break negative cycles in relationships.

How to Incorporate Meditation in Daily Life :

· **Start Small:** Begin with 5-10 minutes of meditation daily, gradually increasing the duration.

· **Focus on the Breath:** Use your breath as an anchor to bring your attention to the present moment.

· **Use Guided Meditations:** If you are new to meditation, apps or online resources can help guide your practice.

· **Practice Gratitude Meditation:** Reflect on the positive aspects of your marriage and express silent gratitude.

Meditation for Self-Awareness

Find a quiet space: Sit in a comfortable, upright posture where you won't be disturbed.

Focus on your breath: Begin by simply observing your breath as it enters and leaves your body. This is grounding and helps bring your awareness to the present moment.

Observe your thoughts: As you meditate, thoughts will naturally arise. Instead of engaging with them, observe them as if you're watching clouds pass by. This practice helps you detach from mental patterns and gain insight into your thought processes.

Practice mindfulness: Focus on the sensations of the body, sounds, and surroundings. Be fully present, without judgment. This allows you to become more aware of your habitual reactions and tendencies.

Pranayama: Harnessing Breath for Emotional Balance

Pranayama, or breath control, is another effective way to achieve self-awareness and emotional balance. By consciously regulating our breath, we can influence our mental state, bringing calmness, clarity, and emotional stability.

Benefits of Pranayama in Marriage

1. **Balances Emotions:** Controlled breathing helps in managing anger, frustration, and stress, leading to healthier communication.

2. **Enhances Mind-Body Awareness:** It increases awareness of bodily sensations and emotional states, helping us recognize and address emotional triggers.

3. **Promotes Relaxation:** Slow and deep breathing activates the parasympathetic nervous system, reducing tension and promoting relaxation.

4. **Encourages Mindful Listening:** When we are calm and centered, we become better listeners, improving overall communication in marriage.

Pranayama for Self-Awareness

Pranayama (breath control) helps in calming the mind and balancing the body's energy, which can enhance self-awareness.

Begin with deep breathing (Dirga Pranayama): Sit comfortably and focus on your breath. Take deep, slow breaths into the abdomen, then the chest, and exhale fully. This will activate the parasympathetic nervous system, calming your mind and making it easier to access deeper layers of awareness.

Nadi Shodhana (Alternate Nostril Breathing): This pranayama helps balance the two hemispheres of the brain, reduces stress, and enhances mental clarity. Close one nostril, inhale through the other, close it, and exhale through the opposite nostril. This practice can calm your mind and help you connect more deeply with your inner self.

Kapalbhati (Skull Shining Breath): This is a more invigorating pranayama, where you focus on forceful exhales and passive inhales. It energizes the body and clears mental fog, fostering greater awareness and presence.

Simple Pranayama Techniques for Self-Awareness

- **Anulom Vilom (Alternate Nostril Breathing):** Helps balance emotions and clears mental clutter.
- **Bhramari (Humming Bee Breath):** Reduces stress and brings inner peace.
- **Ujjayi (Victorious Breath):** Instead of normal chest or shallow breathing, try to have concentrated abdomen breathing while doing Meditation. It enhances focus and emotional stability.
- **Deep Belly Breathing:** Encourages relaxation and mindfulness in daily interactions.

Regular Practice and Integrating Meditation and Pranayama into Your Marriage

Consistency is key: Set aside time daily for meditation and pranayama, even if it's just 10-15 minutes. Over time, this will deepen your self-awareness.

Observe changes in your thought patterns: Notice any shifts in how you react to emotions or situations, which will help you gain deeper insights into your true nature.

Be patient and non-judgmental: Self-awareness takes time to develop. Avoid rushing or forcing it, and instead practice with an open, accepting attitude.

As you continue your practice, you'll begin to notice a more profound connection to your true self, as well as a heightened awareness of the thoughts and emotions that arise. Both meditation and pranayama are powerful tools for exploring your inner world.

- **Practice Together:** Meditating and practicing pranayama as a couple can strengthen your bond and create a shared space of peace and understanding.

- **Use Breathing Techniques During Conflicts:** When emotions run high, taking deep breaths before responding can prevent unnecessary arguments.

- **Set Intentions:** Begin each day with a moment of silence, setting a positive intention for your relationship.

Conclusion

Achieving self-awareness through meditation and pranayama is a transformative journey that enriches both the individual and the marriage. By cultivating inner peace, emotional intelligence, and mindfulness, we create a foundation for a loving, respectful, and harmonious relationship. As you embark on this journey, remember that the key to a fulfilling marriage lies in nurturing your own inner world, allowing you to show up as the best version of yourself for your partner.

Key Takeaways from Part 1:

Understanding yourself is the foundation of building healthy, fulfilling relationships. Self-awareness helps you recognize your emotions, communication patterns, and the underlying needs that shape your interactions. Our past experiences—especially those from childhood and previous relationships—leave lasting imprints, often influencing our relationship dynamics in ways we may not realize. By identifying our personal values, needs, and boundaries, we develop a strong sense of self, ensuring that our relationships are rooted in mutual respect rather than fear, dependency, or compromise.

Achieving self-awareness goes beyond simple reflection; it requires intentional practices like meditation and pranayama, which help calm the mind, regulate emotions, and deepen inner clarity. As we grow in self-understanding, we begin to recognize the hidden patterns that drive our relationships. This brings us to the next essential step: exploring attachment styles and relationship patterns. By understanding these psychological frameworks, we can heal from past wounds, break unhealthy cycles, and build more secure, fulfilling connections.

Part 2

Attachment Styles & Relationship Patterns

Chapters :

5. Overview of attachment theory (secure, anxious, avoidant, fearful-avoidant)
6. How attachment styles impact relationships
7. How to Leverage Individual Differences in Personality Traits for Success
8. Exercises to identify and shift unhealthy patterns

Chapter 5

Understanding Attachment in Relationships

The manner we connect with our partners is moulded by early childhood experiences and encounters with parents and caregivers. Attachment theory, presented by psychologist John Bowlby and further explored by Mary Ainsworth, makes sense of these patterns. Recognizing and identifying your attachment style and that of your partner can help improve understanding and reinforce relationships.

Attachment is a essential aspect of human instinct—a well established need for emotional and physical closeness. From early childhood, we rely on parents and caregivers for security and comfort, shaping to establish the foundation for how we connect with others in adulthood. In marriage, this connection dynamic shift to a spouse, who becomes a primary source of emotional support.

Even as infants, we perceive familiar touches and voices, demonstrating how ingrained the need for attachment is in human relationships. However, what makes attachment particularly fascinating is its uniqueness—no two individuals experience and consequent attachment style is in the exact same manner. While biological factors play a role, attachment and the manner in which we connect, is primarily shaped by early childhood experiences and the emotional surrounding in which we are raised.

Why Attachment Matters in Marriage

Every individual enters a relationship with different emotional needs, assumptions and expectations, but one universal necessity remains: **the need for connection.** In a marriage, this connection involves trust, emotional intimacy, and mutual reliance upon each other.

The Evolution of Attachment

Just as a baby cries when separated from a caregiver or parent, grown-ups too seek reassurance and closeness in relationships by their respective behavior as per attachment style. The need for emotional security doesn't vanish with age—it simply manifests differently.

Even independent individuals who pride themselves on self-sufficiency normally rest on their partners for emotional support and stability. Far from being a sign of weakness, this dependence fosters resilience and strength. A secure marital bond provides a foundation that empowers both partners to grow, pursue their goals, and navigate life's challenges with confidence.

The Four Attachment Styles

The Four Attachment Styles in Marriage

Attachment styles influence emotional connect and intimacy in relationships. They are generally classified into four types: secure, anxious, avoidant, and fearful-avoidant:

1. **Anxious Attachment** – Steady need for reassurance.
2. **Secure Attachment** – Comfortable with intimacy and trust.
3. **Avoidant Attachment** – Inclination for emotional distance.
4. **Fearful-Avoidant Attachment** – Muddled Attachment.

Each style influences how individuals interact with their spouse and respond to conflicts.

In each attachment style, the partners have different and unique attachment roles acting as a secure base. For example, the partner with Anxious Attachment would be engrossed with the relationship and ceaselessly look for his/her partner's time to get reassurance.

The dependency of any of the partners in marriage for seeking proximity and intimacy is not bad. The seed of secured dependency erupts into an aspiration to achieve independence in life. Once, a spouse has a secured base and has a security to fall back to his/her secured base i.e., the other partner, it is always easy to be independent and achieve your goals and aspirations.

An intimate relationship like marriage brings the people together and makes them one. So much so that one can feel the pain of the partner. Such a relationship also brings physiological changes and in a given attachment style can change the BP level of the other spouse. A mere hand-holding can bring down the anxiety level of the other spouse in secure attachment is the true reflection of the fact that marriage (especially in a secure attachment) brings physiological change. In an intimate relationship, each can regulate each other's psychological and emotional wellbeing. I would like to share my own personal experience in this regard.

"I had visited "World of Wonders" at Rohini, Delhi a couple of years back with my wife and kids. One of the joyrides of a giant wheel, my wife sitting next to me got terrified and was under severe stress and immediately grabbed my hand and clutched it throughout the ride. However, later she shared with me that this simple spousal hand-holding helped her to reduce the stress and complete the ride. The physical proximity and availability of partner have influenced the stress response."

Most people have a secure attachment with an almost equal percentage of people having an Anxious and Avoidant Attachment. There may be questions in your mind, as to how one can determine his style of attachment and how it is affecting your relationships.

In the "Marital Attachment Quiz" given below, you can get to know your attachment style. Before heading to that Quiz, Please understand the basic traits and characteristics linked to each attachment style.

1. Anxious Attachment: Seeking Constant Reassurance

Individuals with an **anxious attachment style** seek closeness but tend to worry about their partner's feelings and fear abandonment. They may rely heavily on their partner's continuous validation and reassurance. They often may overanalyze interactions, which can lead to emotional ups and downs.

Example:

Neha and Arjun have been married for three years. If Arjun doesn't reply to Neha's texts within an hour, she immediately assumes he's upset or losing interest. She sends multiple messages, feeling restless until she gets a response. Arjun, unaware of her underlying fears, feels overwhelmed by her constant need for reassurance.

Common Traits:

- Highly sensitive to their partner's actions and moods

- Overanalyzing partner's words and actions.
- Fear of being abandoned
- Need for constant reassurance
- Emotional highs and lows

Impact on Relationships:

This can create challenges if one partner struggles to meet emotional needs. For example, A couple, I worked with had similar challenges—Ravi would call his wife multiple times a day, worried that she might be upset with him. His constant need for validation strained their bond until they got counseling to work on building trust and open communication.

2. Secure Attachment: The Foundation of a Healthy Marriage

Securely attached individuals are comfortable with emotional intimacy, trust, and communication. They navigate conflicts constructively and don't view disagreements as threats to the relationship.

Example:

When Priya and Karan have a disagreement, Karan calmly says, **"Let's take a break and talk when we're both relaxed."** Instead of escalating conflicts, they focus on finding solutions together.

Common Traits:

- Confident in their partner's love and commitment.
- Open to discussing emotions and concerns.
- Approaching disagreements with patience and understanding.
- Comfortable with emotional closeness
- Honest and open in communication
- Confidence in self-worth

Impact on Relationships:

Securely attached individuals create stable, supportive relationships. For example, A client once shared that her husband always reassured her by holding her hand during difficult conversations. This small gesture made her feels safe, reinforcing their emotional bond.

3. Avoidant Attachment: Guarding Emotional Independence

People with an **avoidant attachment style** struggle with emotional closeness and may resist dependency in relationships. While they care deeply, they often withdraw when situations demand vulnerability.

Example:

Mehul loves his wife, Aditi, but finds it difficult to express affection. When Aditi wants to discuss their emotional connection, Mehul often changes the subject or downplays her concerns. Over time, Aditi begins feeling emotionally distant, even though Mehul doesn't intend to push her away.

Common Traits:

- Difficulty expressing emotions.
- Preferring independence over emotional closeness.
- Struggling with commitment and vulnerability
- Tendency to withdraw during conflicts
- Have preference for autonomy

Impact on Relationships:

Partners may feel emotionally distant or unsupported. For example, One couple I counseled had a wife who was avoidant in her attachment. She often dismissed her husband's need for emotional closeness, seeing it as "clingy." Over time, she realized her childhood experiences shaped this reaction, and with conscious effort, she began embracing emotional intimacy.

4. Fearful-Avoidant Attachment - Muddled or Disorganized Attachment

This style combines anxious and avoidant tendencies, leading to mixed signals in relationships.

Common Traits:

- Desire for closeness but fear of emotional pain
- Conflicted feelings about intimacy
- Difficulty trusting others
- Fluctuations between seeking closeness and withdrawing

Impact on Relationships:

Emotional instability can make it hard to build trust. Aisha wants a deep connection with Kabir but often pulls away, creating confusion.

The Role of Attachment in Emotional Well-Being

Marriage is more than a partnership—it's a **source of emotional regulation and connect.** Spouses influence each other's psychological well-being, often without realizing it.

Example:

After a stressful day, Raj comes home feeling overwhelmed. Without saying much, his wife Rhea hugs him. That simple act lowers his stress levels and reassures him that he's not alone.

Small Gestures That Reinforce Attachment:

- Holding hands during difficult times/conversations.
- Expressing appreciation through small notes or compliments.
- Being emotionally present, even in silence.

Can Attachment Styles Change?

Yes! While attachment styles Aka personality are shaped by early experiences, they are **not permanent.** One can work upon, although it might takes more than couple of years to bring a satisfactory change. Through self-awareness, therapy, and positive relationship experiences, individuals can move toward a **more secure attachment style.**

Ways to Foster a Secure Attachment in Marriage:

1. **Increase Emotional Awareness** – Recognize patterns in your attachment behaviors.
2. **Communicate Openly** – Share concerns and feelings without fear of judgment.
3. **Reassure Each Other** – Simple affirmations can strengthen emotional security.
4. **Work Through Conflicts Constructively** – Focus on problem-solving rather than blaming.

Discover Your Attachment Style

Are you curious about your attachment style? Take the **Marital Attachment Quiz** below to gain insights into how you navigate relationships. Understanding your attachment style can be the first step toward creating a healthier, more fulfilling marriage.

MARITAL ATTACHMENT QUIZ

Understand Your Attachment Style for a Stronger Relationship

---

1. How Do You Feel About Emotional Closeness?

□ **Choose the statement that resonates most with you:**

◆ **A.** I feel comfortable forming close bonds with my partner.

◆ **B.** I sometimes struggle with emotional intimacy and prefer keeping some distance.

◆ **C.** I crave deep closeness, but I often feel my partner doesn't match my level of attachment.

---

2. How Do You Handle Dependence in a Relationship?

💡 **Select the option that best describes your comfort level with relying on your partner:**

◆ **A.** I trust my partner and feel secure depending on them as much as they rely on me.

◆ **B.** I find it hard to fully trust and depend on my partner.

◆ **C.** I frequently worry that my partner doesn't love me enough or might leave me.

---

3. How Do You Respond to Relationship Anxiety?

💬 **What describes your reaction to emotional security and attachment?**

◆ **A.** I rarely worry about my partner leaving or becoming too emotionally close.
◆ **B.** I get uncomfortable when my partner seeks too much emotional closeness.
◆ **C.** I desire deep connection and sometimes fear it might push my partner away.

What Your Answers Reveal About You

● **Mostly A's:** You have a **secure attachment style**, meaning you navigate relationships with trust and ease.
□ **Mostly B's:** You may have an **avoidant attachment style**, where independence is your priority, but intimacy can feel challenging.
● **Mostly C's:** You likely have an **anxious attachment style**, where deep connection is essential to you, but worries about rejection may arise.

Discover ways to enhance your relationship by understanding your attachment style!
For personalized insights, visit: [www.legalmindajitkumar.com]

If you have any thoughts or questions, feel free to share—I'd be happy to guide you on this journey of self-discovery and relationship growth!

Strengthening Relationships Through Attachment Awareness

Recognizing attachment styles can improve relationship dynamics. Here are some ways to nurture a healthy connection:

1. **Identify Your Attachment Style:** Reflect on your emotional patterns and behaviors.

2. **Communicate Openly:** Discuss attachment tendencies with your partner for better understanding.

3. **Practice Emotional Regulation:** Manage insecurities through mindfulness, self-reflection, or therapy.

4. **Build a Supportive Environment:** Offer reassurance, respect emotional needs, and foster trust.

5. **Seek Professional Support:** Therapy can help address deep-rooted attachment issues.

Attachment theory is not just about understanding ourselves—it's about **cultivating empathy for our partners.** Recognizing and respecting each other's emotional need allows couples to bridge communication gaps, reduce conflicts, and build deeper intimacy.

Whether you naturally seek reassurance, cherish emotional closeness, or struggle with vulnerability, remember that relationships thrive on **growth, patience, and mutual understanding.** With the right effort, any couple can build a **secure, loving, and lasting** marriage.

Your attachment style influences your relationships, but it does not define them. Understanding these patterns can help couples build deeper connections, improve communication, and create a lasting, healthy partnership.

Chapter 6

How Attachment Styles Impact Relationships

An attachment style assumes a significant role in shaping how we connect with our partners. These styles are framed in childhood, based on our early experiences with parents or caregivers, which is being reflected in our unique personality distinct from others. Our Attachment style Aka personality continue to influence how we express love, handle conflicts, and seek emotional support in adulthood. Understanding your attachment style or personality and that of your partner can help build a stronger and more fulfilling marriage.

How Attachment Styles Affect Marriage

Each attachment style—secure, anxious, avoidant, and fearful-avoidant—shapes how people approach intimacy, trust, and communication. Recognizing these patterns in yourself and your spouse can help create a more understanding and harmonious relationship.

1. Secure Attachment: The Foundation of a Healthy Marriage

People with a secure attachment style are comfortable with emotional closeness, communicate openly, and trust their partners. They balance independence with connection, making them dependable and emotionally supportive.

Example: Aarav and Meera have been married for five years. Whenever they have disagreements, they listen to each other, express their concerns without fear, and find solutions together. Their trust in each other helps them navigate difficult times with ease.

Impact on Marriage:

- Healthy communication and conflict resolution
- Deep trust and emotional security
- Comfort in expressing emotions and needs
- Strong emotional and physical intimacy

2. Anxious Attachment: Fear of Abandonment

People with an anxious attachment style crave closeness but often fear rejection. They may constantly seek reassurance from their partner and become anxious if they sense emotional distance.

Example: Priya often worries that her husband, Rohit, does not love her enough. If he takes longer than usual to respond to a message, she starts overthinking and feels insecure. This sometimes leads to unnecessary arguments, making Rohit feel pressured.

Impact on Marriage:

- Frequent need for validation and reassurance
- Intense emotional reactions to perceived neglect
- Difficulty trusting partner's commitment
- Overanalyzing partner's words and actions

How to Improve:

- Practicing self-soothing techniques to manage anxiety
- Developing trust through open and consistent communication
- Recognizing personal self-worth beyond the relationship

3. Avoidant Attachment: The Fear of Dependence

People with an avoidant attachment style value independence and often struggle with emotional closeness. They may suppress their feelings and withdraw when faced with stress or deep emotional conversations.

Example: Raj loves his wife, Kavya, but he finds it difficult to express his emotions. When she tries to talk about their relationship, he avoids the conversation or dismisses her concerns, leaving her feeling unimportant.

Impact on Marriage:

- Difficulty expressing emotions or being vulnerable
- Avoidance of deep emotional discussions
- Tendency to withdraw during conflicts
- Preferring personal space over emotional connection

How to Improve:

- Practicing small steps to open up emotionally
- Understanding that vulnerability strengthens relationships
- Learning to balance independence with emotional intimacy

4. Fearful-Avoidant Attachment: The Push-Pull Dynamic

People with a fearful-avoidant attachment style exhibit both anxious and avoidant tendencies. They want emotional closeness but fear getting hurt, leading to mixed signals in relationships.

Example: Sneha wants to feel close to her husband, Arjun, but the moment he gets too emotionally available, she pushes him away. She fears that if she depends on him too much, she might end up hurt, creating a cycle of emotional ups and downs.

Impact on Marriage:

- Alternating between seeking intimacy and withdrawing
- Struggles with trust and emotional regulation
- Fear of getting hurt but also craving connection
- Unstable emotional patterns in relationships

How to Improve:

- Seeking professional support to address past trauma
- Building trust through open and transparent communication
- Developing emotional regulation skills

Working Together on Attachment Differences

Every couple experiences differences in their attachment styles, but understanding these patterns can help improve relationships. Here's how:

1. **Communicate Openly:** Talk about your attachment tendencies and how they affect your relationship.

2. **Practice Emotional Awareness:** Recognize your emotional triggers and work on self-regulation.

3. **Be Patient and Empathetic:** Understand that changing attachment behaviors takes time and effort.

4. **Seek Professional Help if Needed:** Therapy, counseling or relationship coaching can provide guidance in managing attachment-related challenges.

Conclusion

Your attachment style shapes how you connect with your partner, but it does not define your future. By understanding your behaviors and working towards a more secure attachment, you can create a relationship built on trust, intimacy, and emotional resilience. A fulfilling marriage is about mutual respect, love, and continuous effort to grow together.

Chapter 7

How to Leverage Individual Differences in Personality Traits for Success

Every individual is unique, molded by a combination of psychological and physiological traits. While physical attributes are effectively discernible and visible, psychological attributes assume a more prominent role in shaping our identity and influencing how we engage with the world. These traits contribute to diverse reactions to similar situations, making personality a key factor in personal and professional development. Understanding and embracing these differences can help individuals unlock their potential and achieve succcss. Let's explore how it works.

Understanding Individual Differences

No two individuals are identical. While similarities exist, distinct traits set people apart, incorporating personality, intelligence, interests, and aptitudes. Perceiving these underline differences allows individuals to align their strengths with their aspirations.

Perceiving individual differences relies on two key principles:

· **Reliability**: Ensuring that a trait is consistently measured over time.

· **Validity**: Confirming that a test accurately assesses the intended characteristic.

Among various human attributes, personality stands out as a crucial factor in predicting behavior and understanding uniqueness.

The Nature of Personality

Personality refers to an individual's consistent patterns of thought, emotion, and behavior. It evolves through a combination of unconscious needs, social and cultural influences, personal experiences, and potential for growth. Gordon Allport (1937) famously described personality as *"the dynamic organization within the individual of those psychological systems that determine their unique adjustment to the environment."*

Personality is influenced by several factors:

1. **Unconscious needs and internal conflicts**: These often stem from early life experiences.

2. **Socio-cultural environment**: The society and culture in which an individual grows up shape their outlook and behavior.

3. **Life experiences**: Personal challenges and achievements leave lasting impressions.

4. **Potential for growth**: Every individual has the innate ability to evolve and adapt.

Personality, therefore, is a dynamic and multifaceted aspect of human psychology. As a dynamic aspect of psychology, personality can be examined through established models such as the Five-Factor Model, also known as the "Big Five" or "OCEAN."

The Big Five Personality Traits (OCEAN)

The Five-Factor Model categorizes personality traits into five broad domains, offering a structured way to understand individual differences. Each domain encompasses specific attributes, and together, they provide a comprehensive view of personality.

1. Openness to Experience

This trait reflects a person's openness to exploring new ideas, embracing creativity, and seeking unconventional experiences.

There are 6 other sub traits under this domain of openness to experience, which are: a). Imagination, b).

Artistic interests, c). Emotionality, d). Adventurousness, e). Intellect, and f). Liberalism.

High Openness: Individuals high in this trait are imaginative, curious, and willing to step out of their comfort zones. Such individuals are high on this scale are reflective, creative, innovative, imaginative and an untraditional and are persons open to trying new ideas. They are not close-minded individuals instead they are imaginative and curious characters, analytical and such characteristics are positively related to intelligence.

For example, a scientist developing groundbreaking theories or an artist experimenting with new mediums embodies openness. Think of Steve Jobs, whose innovative mindset revolutionized technology.

Low Openness: On the other hand, those low in openness prefer routine and familiarity. They are pragmatic and focused on practical solutions. For instance, an accountant who values established procedures over creative approaches may score low on this trait.

Example: Consider an entrepreneur launching a startup in an untested market. Their openness allows them to innovate, adapt, and thrive in uncertainty, while a team member low in openness might excel in stabilizing operations and managing risks.

2. Conscientiousness

This trait measures an individual's level of organization, responsibility, and goal orientation.

· **High Conscientiousness**: People high in this trait are disciplined, hardworking, and dependable. For example, a project manager who meets every deadline and ensures the team's success reflects conscientiousness. Athletes like Serena Williams, known for their dedication and persistence, exemplify this trait.

· **Low Conscientiousness**: Those low in this trait may struggle with procrastination or lack of focus, thriving better in unstructured environments. Creative writers, for instance, may intentionally work in bursts of inspiration rather than following strict schedules.

Example: A conscientious student who methodically prepares for exams often outperforms peers who rely on last-minute cramming, showcasing the importance of planning and persistence.

3. Extraversion

Extraversion captures the extent to which an individual is outgoing, energetic, and socially engaged.

· **High Extraversion**: Extroverts thrive in social settings, drawing energy from interactions. For example, a charismatic salesperson closing deals with ease demonstrates high extraversion. Politicians like

Barack Obama, known for their dynamic public presence, are prime examples.

· **Low Extraversion (Introversion)**: Introverts, on the other hand, are more reflective and prefer deeper, one-on-one interactions. A software developer who excels in solitary problem-solving rather than group brainstorming might score low on extraversion.

Example: A team of event organizers might benefit from the extrovert's enthusiasm to engage clients and the introvert's attention to behind-the-scenes details.

4. Agreeableness

This trait reflects a person's tendency to be compassionate, cooperative, and altruistic.

· **High Agreeableness**: Highly agreeable individuals are empathetic, team-oriented, and willing to help others. Nurses, teachers, and social workers often exemplify this trait.

· **Low Agreeableness**: Those low in agreeableness may prioritize self-interest, sometimes to the detriment of others. While this might sound negative, it can be beneficial in competitive fields such as corporate negotiations.

Example: A high-agreeableness teacher fosters a nurturing classroom environment, while a low-agreeableness entrepreneur focuses on tough decision-making to grow their business.

5. Neuroticism

Neuroticism measures emotional stability and the likelihood of experiencing negative emotions such as anxiety and mood swings.

· **High Neuroticism**: People high in this trait may struggle with stress and self-doubt. Artists like Vincent van Gogh, who channeled emotional turbulence into creativity, are notable examples.

· **Low Neuroticism**: Those low in neuroticism are calm, resilient, and emotionally stable. For instance, a surgeon performing under high-pressure conditions requires low neuroticism to maintain focus.

Example: During a crisis, a leader with low neuroticism can inspire confidence and stability, while a team member with high neuroticism might need additional support to manage stress.

Applying Personality Insights for Success

Understanding personality traits isn't just theoretical; it has practical applications that can drive success in multiple areas:

1. **Personal Growth**: Recognizing your strengths and areas for improvement enables targeted self-development. For example, an introvert can work on communication skills to excel in leadership roles.

2. **Career Alignment**: Matching personality traits to job roles enhances performance. A creative individual high in openness might thrive in design, while a conscientious person excels in roles requiring precision, such as accounting.

3. **Team Building**: Awareness of team members' traits fosters collaboration. A balance of extroverts, introverts, and conscientious planners can create a well-rounded team.

4. **Decision-Making**: Leaders who understand personality differences can tailor their communication and motivate individuals effectively. For instance, an extraverted manager might energize their team through engaging speeches, while an introverted one focuses on personalized feedback.

Example: In a startup environment, an extroverted founder might attract investors, while their conscientious co-founder ensures smooth operations.

Conclusion

Embracing individual personality differences fosters growth, enhances teamwork, and paves the way for success. By applying insights from the Big Five framework, individuals and organizations can make informed decisions, maximize potential, and create environments where diverse traits complement each other. Recognizing and leveraging these unique characteristics ultimately leads to greater fulfillment and achievement in both personal and professional spheres.

Chapter 8

Exercises to Identify and Shift Unhealthy Patterns

Relationships thrive when partners are mindful of their behaviors through understanding personality traits or attachment style and actively work towards growth. Recognizing and shifting unhealthy patterns requires self-reflection, intentional effort, and practical exercises to bring enduring change. This chapter provides noteworthy steps to help couples identify destructive habits and replace them with healthier alternatives, with relatable examples from Indian relationships.

1. Self-Reflection Journaling

Objective: Understand personal behaviors and patterns that affect the relationship.

Example: Priya noticed that every time her husband Rohan came home late from work, she became irritable and distant. Through journaling, she understood her reaction originated from childhood experiences of feeling ignored by her busy parents.

- Spend 10-15 minutes everyday writing about moments when you felt triggered, defensive, or misjudged.

- Reflect on how your reactions influenced the interaction with your partner. Try to analyze, if there was any contribution on your part leading to a particular situation.
- Identify recurring themes and consider the root cause of these emotions.

2. The Mirror Exercise

Objective: Increase self-awareness by observing and noticing personal responses in conflict situations.

Example: Arjun and Meera often argued about household chores. One day, Arjun tried this exercise and noticed his dismissive tone when responding to Meera's concerns. This realization helped him communicate more respectfully.

- Stand in front of a mirror and recall a recent argument.
- Verbally replay your words and observe your tone, facial expressions, and body language.
- Ask yourself: "Would I be comfortable if my partner spoke to me this way?"
- Adjust your approach based on what you learn.

3. Role Reversal Exercise

Objective: Encourage empathy and understanding.

Example: Amit and Neha frequently clashed over Neha's long phone calls with her family. They decided to switch roles—Amit had to justify why he needed to talk to his mother, while Neha needed to make sense of how she felt disregarded during those calls. This helped them appreciate each other's feelings.

- Choose a recurring conflict and swap roles with your partner.
- Each partner expresses the other's perspective as accurately as possible.
- Afterward, discuss what it felt like to be in the other's shoes and what insights were gained.

4. Pattern Mapping

Objective: Identify recurring negative cycles and replace them with healthier and better responses.

Example: Kavya and Sanjay realized they generally fought when discussing finances. Mapping their arguments showed that fear and insecurity were at the root of their conflicts, leading them to approach monetary discussions with more patience and understanding.

- Draw a simple flowchart of a typical argument or tension point.
- Note what triggers the pattern and how both partners respond.
- Brainstorm alternative, healthier responses and write them next to the original reactions.
- Commit to implementing one positive change during the next conflict.

5. The Pause and Breathe Method

Objective: Break the cycle of impulsive reactions and encourage mindful responses.

Example: Rajesh, who had a habit of keeping high pitch voice during arguments, started pausing and taking deep breaths before responding. Over time, this helped him communicate in a calmer and more constructive manner.

- When feeling triggered, take a deep breath and pause for five seconds before responding.
- Ask yourself: "Is my response constructive or reactive?"
- If needed, take a break before continuing the conversation.

6. Weekly Check-ins

Objective: Create an organized space for growth and communication.

Example: Sita and Manoj set aside every Sunday evening to discuss their relationship. This routine allowed them to celebrate progress, address concerns, and stay emotionally connected.

- Set aside 30 minutes each week to discuss relationship patterns.
- Each partner shares one personal habit they are working on.

- Acknowledge progress, provide support, and set new expectations for the upcoming week.

Conclusion

Unhealthy relationship patterns are often deeply ingrained but can be transformed with awareness and effort. By regularly practicing these exercises, couples can cultivate healthier responses, strengthen their bond, and create a relationship rooted in mutual respect and understanding. Awareness is the first step toward change, and each small shift brings a marriage closer to harmony and fulfillment.

Key Takeaways from Part 2:

Our attachment styles play a fundamental role in shaping our relationships. Whether secure, anxious, avoidant, or fearful-avoidant, these patterns influence how we express affection, handle disagreements, and navigate emotional closeness. Gaining insight into our own attachment style—and recognizing those of others—enables us to break free from unhelpful habits and cultivate stronger, healthier connections.

In addition to attachment, personality differences also impact relationships. Instead of viewing these differences as challenges, embracing them can lead to greater understanding and harmony. By engaging in self-reflection and targeted exercises, we can pinpoint unproductive patterns and actively work toward more fulfilling interactions.

However, self-awareness alone does not lead to change. The next step is developing emotional intelligence and self-regulation—skills that help us manage emotions, communicate effectively, and respond with thoughtfulness rather than impulse. In the next chapter, we will explore how emotional intelligence strengthens relationships, improves conflict resolution, and deepens emotional connection.

Part 3

Emotional Intelligence & Self-Regulation

Chapters:

9. Understanding emotions and their triggers
10. 5 C's of Social Skills for a Thriving Relationship
11. The role of self-regulation in relationship harmony
12. Practical exercises for emotional mastery

Chapter 9

Understanding Emotions and Their Triggers

Emotions play a crucial role in shaping relationships, influencing and shaping patterns how partners communicate, connect, and respond to each other. They serve as the foundation for intimacy, mutual trust and understanding making them fundamental for healthy relationship. When emotions are acknowledged and managed effectively, they tend to strengthen the connection and promote emotional balance and security. Understanding emotions and their triggers helps couples develop empathy, manage conflicts better, and build a stronger bond. This chapter explores the impact of emotions in relationships and provides practical strategies to identify and handle emotional triggers.

1. The Role of Emotions in Relationships:

Recognize how emotions influence interactions and relationship dynamics

- Emotions act as signals, guiding responses and decisions.

• Identifying feelings like frustration, joy, or insecurity helps partners respond thoughtfully instead of impulsively.

• Practicing Emotional awareness fosters meaningful conversations by being mindful of one's emotions. It helps in deeper understanding of their triggers, which help in responding rather than reacting on impulse.

2. Identifying Personal Emotional Triggers:

Recognize what causes intense emotional reactions.

• Reflect on past arguments and note what specifically triggered strong feelings.

• Common triggers include feeling ignored, disrespected, or unappreciated.

• Recognizing triggers helps prevent unnecessary misunderstandings and conflicts.

Example: Meera often feels hurt when Raj forgets to acknowledge her efforts at home. She realizes her emotional trigger stems from growing up in a family where appreciation was rarely expressed.

3. The Impact of Childhood and Past Experiences :

Understand how past experiences shape emotional responses.

- Many emotional triggers come from childhood or previous relationships.
- Identifying old patterns can help avoid repeating unhealthy cycles.
- Sharing past experiences with your partner builds trust and deeper understanding.

Example: Arjun becomes defensive whenever his wife Priya questions his financial decisions. Reflecting on his past, he realizes that his parents frequently argued about money, making him extra sensitive to financial discussions.

4. Recognizing Emotional Patterns in Conflict:

Observe emotional responses during arguments to uncover repeating patterns.

- Notice common themes in conflicts and recurring emotional reactions.

• Pay attention to physical signals like a racing heart or clenched fists, which indicate emotional stress.

• Use this awareness to approach conflicts more calmly and mindfully.

Example: During arguments, Neha tends to shut down and avoid discussion. She realizes this stems from a childhood habit of staying silent to avoid punishment. Acknowledging this helps her work on open communication with her husband, Rohan.

5. Responding vs. Reacting Objective:

Shift from reactive emotional responses to thoughtful engagement.

• Pause before responding to heated situations.

• Practice deep breathing or counting to ten before speaking.

• Frame responses positively (e.g., "I feel hurt when..." instead of "You never listen!").

Example: When Amit forgets to call, Pooja used to react angrily. Now, she takes a deep breath, expresses her feelings calmly, and avoids escalating the argument.

6. Communicating Emotions Effectively:

Express emotions in a way that strengthens connection and avoids misinterpretation.

• Use "I" statements to express feelings without blaming (e.g., "I feel sad when you cancel plans.")

• Acknowledge your partner's emotions, even if you see things differently.

• Encourage open discussions about emotions to build a safe space for communication.

7. Exercises for Emotional Awareness:

Build emotional intelligence through daily practice of empathy, active listening, and self-regulation.

• Emotion Tracking Journal: Write down emotions and their triggers every day.

• Mindfulness Meditation: Stay present with emotions without reacting impulsively.

• Partner Check-ins: Have regular conversations about emotions and triggers in a calm, supportive way.

Conclusion

Understanding emotions and their triggers is essential for a healthy relationship. By practicing emotional awareness, recognizing past patterns, and improving communication, couples can build stronger connections, deeper empathy, and resilience. When emotions are handled thoughtfully, they become a tool for growth rather than a cause of conflict.

Chapter 10

5 C's of Social Skills for a Thriving Relationship

From childhood, we start learning about relationships through our interactions with family, friends, and eventually, romantic partners. These early experiences shape how we understand connections and help us navigate the complexities of relationships.

As we grow, we engage in different types of relationships—friendships, romantic partnerships, and marriages. To sustain a healthy and fulfilling relationship, certain social skills are essential, especially in marriage, where communication, patience, and mutual effort play a crucial role.

Here are the **5 C's of Social Skills** that can help you strengthen your bond:

---

1. Consciousness: Understanding Emotions and Perspectives

A strong relationship begins with self-awareness. Recognizing your emotions and understanding how they influence your reactions can improve the way you interact with your partner. When you are conscious of your thoughts and feelings, it becomes easier to manage conflicts and build deeper emotional connections.

Example:

Sonia and Rohan, a newlywed couple, often clashed over small misunderstandings. Sonia would feel upset when Rohan didn't respond to her messages immediately, assuming he was ignoring her. Rohan, on the other hand, was simply caught up at work. Once Sonia became aware of her insecurities and Rohan acknowledged her need for reassurance, they found ways to bridge the gap—such as Rohan sending a quick message when busy and Sonia practicing patience.

How to develop consciousness:

- Regularly reflect on your emotions and responses.
- Identify what triggers stress or insecurity in your relationship.
- Observe your partner's emotional patterns to understand their needs better.

---

2. Composure: Staying Balanced During Conflicts

Disagreements are inevitable, but how you handle them can define the strength of your relationship. Keeping your emotions in check and responding calmly rather than reacting impulsively can prevent small issues from escalating into major conflicts.

Example:

During a festival gathering, Aman and Priya found themselves arguing over how to manage expenses. Instead of raising his voice or walking away, Aman took a deep breath and calmly explained his concerns. Priya, noticing his composure, also softened her tone. Their ability to stay calm helped them find a solution without turning the disagreement into a fight.

Tips to maintain composure:

- Take a pause before responding during heated moments.
- Focus on the issue, not the person—avoid personal attacks.
- Practice deep breathing or mindfulness techniques to stay centered.

Remaining composed allows discussions to be productive rather than destructive.

---

3. Communication: The Foundation of Every Relationship

Clear and respectful communication is vital for any lasting relationship. It ensures both partners feel heard and valued, reducing misunderstandings and fostering emotional intimacy.

Example:

Anjali and Dev had different love languages—Anjali valued words of affirmation, while Dev showed love through actions. Initially, Anjali felt unappreciated because Dev wasn't expressive with words. When they openly discussed their needs, Dev made an effort to express his feelings verbally, while Anjali began recognizing and appreciating Dev's actions.

Ways to improve communication:

- Listen attentively instead of preparing a response while your partner speaks.
- Use "I" statements instead of "You always" or "You never" to avoid blame.
- Clarify misunderstandings rather than assuming intentions.

A strong relationship thrives on honest, thoughtful, and clear communication.

---

4. Collaboration: Supporting Each Other as a Team

A relationship isn't about competition; it's about teamwork. Supporting each other's dreams, sharing responsibilities, and making joint decisions strengthen the partnership.

Example:

Raj and Simran both had demanding jobs but wanted to maintain a healthy work-life balance. Instead of expecting one person to manage household duties, they divided tasks—Raj handled grocery shopping and morning chores, while Simran managed cooking and laundry. Their teamwork made daily life smoother and strengthened their bond.

How to practice collaboration:

- Regularly check in with your partner about shared responsibilities.
- Encourage and support each other's career or personal goals.
- Approach challenges together rather than shifting blame.

A collaborative mindset fosters a relationship where both partners feel equally valued and supported.

---

5. Compassion: Cultivating Empathy and Understanding

Compassion means being kind and considerate toward your partner's emotions and struggles. It requires setting aside ego, understanding their perspective, and offering support when needed.

Example:

When Meera lost a big business deal, she was upset and withdrawn. Instead of telling her to "move on," her husband, Arjun, simply sat with her, listened, and reassured her that setbacks were part of growth. His compassionate response made Meera feel supported rather than judged.

Ways to practice compassion:

- Validate your partner's emotions, even if you don't fully understand them.
- Show kindness in small ways—like a heartfelt note, a hug, or simply listening.
- Be patient and forgiving, acknowledging that everyone has difficult days.

Compassion deepens emotional connection and strengthens the foundation of trust in a relationship.

Overcoming Tough Times Together

Every relationship faces challenges—be it financial struggles, external stress, or personal conflicts. Those who cultivate the right social skills are better equipped to navigate difficult periods without damaging their bond.

Strategies to stay connected during hardships:

- **Increase communication** – If face-to-face discussions become difficult, try writing notes or texts to express feelings.
- **Engage in shared activities** – Whether it's cooking together or taking an evening walk, small shared moments strengthen connection.
- **Prioritize emotional well-being** – Practicing meditation, journaling, or seeking professional help can contribute to a healthier mindset for both partners.

By facing difficulties together with patience and understanding, relationships grow even stronger.

Final Thoughts

Healthy relationships require effort, but by practicing **Consciousness, Composure, Communication, Collaboration, and Compassion**, you can create a loving and supportive partnership that stands the test of time.

No relationship is perfect, but when both partners commit to growth and understanding, they build a bond that thrives through every season of life.

Chapter 11

The Role of Self-Regulation in Relationship Harmony

A successful marriage isn't just about love and communication—it also requires emotional self-regulation. The ability to manage emotions, thoughts, and reactions helps maintain harmony in a relationship. When both partners practice self-regulation, they create a peaceful and supportive environment where they feel respected, valued, and understood. This chapter explores why self-regulation is crucial and provides practical ways to develop this skill.

1. Understanding Self-Regulation

Objective: Define self-regulation and its impact on relationships.

- Self-regulation means controlling emotional reactions, impulses, and behaviors instead of reacting impulsively.
- It prevents unnecessary conflicts by encouraging thoughtful responses.
- A partner who can regulate emotions helps maintain a stable and positive relationship dynamic.

Example: Imagine Rajesh comes home tired from work, and Priya asks him to help with household chores. If Rajesh immediately snaps, saying, "Can't you see I'm exhausted?" an argument might follow. But if he pauses, breathes, and responds, "I had a tough day—can I help after a short break?" he avoids unnecessary tension. This is self-regulation in action.

2. The Link Between Emotional Control and Relationship Stability

Objective: Understand how emotional regulation fosters trust and connection.

- Frequent emotional outbursts can weaken trust and intimacy.
- Managing emotions helps partners handle disagreements calmly.
- Emotional stability reassures both individuals, making it easier to share feelings and concerns openly.

Example: When Ananya and Vivek argue, Vivek tends to withdraw and stop talking. Ananya misinterprets this as indifference and gets more upset. Instead, if Vivek calmly explains, "I need some time to process before I can talk," it prevents misunderstandings and helps them resolve issues effectively.

3. Identifying Emotional Triggers

Objective: Recognize personal triggers that may lead to reactive behavior.

- Reflect on past arguments to identify what made emotions escalate.
- Common triggers include feeling ignored, disrespected, or criticized.
- Recognizing triggers allows partners to address issues proactively.

Example: If Arjun notices that he becomes irritated when his wife Neha corrects him in front of others, he can acknowledge this trigger and calmly communicate his feelings later instead of reacting in the moment.

4. Strategies for Strengthening Self-Regulation

Objective: Learn techniques to manage emotions effectively.

- **Pause Before Reacting:** When emotions run high, take a deep breath and count to ten before responding.
- **Practice Mindfulness:** Meditation or deep breathing exercises can help increase emotional awareness.
- **Journaling:** Writing down emotions can provide clarity and prevent impulsive reactions.

- **Self-Soothing Techniques:** Listen to music, go for a walk, or practice gratitude to calm down before responding.

Example: Instead of arguing immediately when upset, Meera steps away, takes a few deep breaths, and reminds herself, "I want to solve the issue, not make it worse." This small practice helps her handle conflicts with more patience.

5. The Role of Self-Regulation in Conflict Resolution

Objective: Apply self-regulation techniques during disagreements.

- Instead of raising your voice, express concerns calmly.
- If emotions escalate, take a break and return to the conversation later with a clearer mind.
- Use "I" statements to avoid blame (e.g., "I feel hurt when…" instead of "You always…").

Example: When Sameer forgets their anniversary, instead of shouting, "You never care about me!" his wife Kavya says, "I felt really disappointed when you forgot our anniversary. I would love it if we could celebrate together this weekend." This approach prevents conflict from escalating.

6. Encouraging Mutual Growth

Objective: Foster a relationship where both partners practice self-regulation.

- Support each other during stressful moments by offering reassurance instead of criticism.
- Make self-regulation a shared goal in your relationship.
- Set aside time to reflect on emotional well-being together.

Example: Instead of blaming each other when feeling overwhelmed, Aditya and Riya take a few minutes each day to check in and share their emotions. This habit strengthens their bond and helps them regulate their emotions as a team.

Conclusion

Self-regulation is a powerful tool for maintaining relationship harmony. By learning to manage emotions and reactions, couples can reduce unnecessary conflicts, strengthen their bond, and create a peaceful and loving partnership. When both partners take responsibility for their emotional responses, they build a marriage based on mutual respect, patience, and long-term happiness.

When you learn to manage your emotions and respond with patience rather than react impulsively, you create a more stable and understanding relationship. Self-regulation helps in preventing unnecessary conflicts, fostering trust, and maintaining harmony. However, managing emotions is just one part of the journey—truly thriving in a relationship requires a deeper understanding of your emotions and the ability to express them in a healthy way. In the next chapter, we will explore emotional mastery, offering practical techniques to help you navigate your feelings with confidence and build a stronger emotional bond with your partner.

Chapter 12

Practical Exercises for Emotional Mastery

Emotional mastery is essential for a happy and lasting marriage. It helps individuals understand, regulate, and express their emotions in a healthy way, leading to better communication and a stronger connection. Developing emotional mastery takes practice, patience, and self-awareness. This chapter introduces practical exercises to help individuals and couples strengthen emotional intelligence and maintain balance in their relationship.

1. The Emotional Awareness Journal

Objective: Recognize and track emotional patterns.

· Dedicate a few minutes each day to writing about your emotions and what triggered them.

· Identify situations that led to strong emotional reactions, whether positive or negative.

· Reflect on how these emotions influenced your interactions with your partner.

· Look for recurring themes—are certain words, actions, or situations consistently affecting your emotions?

Example: Priya noticed she often felt irritated when her husband, Raj, came home late without informing her. Through journaling, she realized this stemmed from childhood experiences of feeling ignored. Recognizing this helped her communicate her feelings calmly instead of reacting with anger.

2. The Pause-and-Breathe Technique

Objective: Develop impulse control and thoughtful responses.

- When emotions start to rise, take a deep breath and count to five before reacting.
- Focus on slow, deep breathing to calm your mind and body.
- Ask yourself: *Is my reaction helping or hurting the situation?*
- Respond only after regaining emotional balance.

Example: Amit and Neha often argued about finances. One evening, Neha got upset over an unexpected expense. Instead of immediately defending himself, Amit took a deep breath and calmly explained why he made the purchase. This simple pause prevented a heated argument.

3. The Emotion Naming Exercise

Objective: Enhance self-awareness and effective communication.

· Instead of saying, *"I'm upset,"* try specifying the exact emotion, such as *"I'm frustrated," "I'm anxious,"* or *"I'm disappointed."*

· Discuss emotions openly with your partner to foster mutual understanding.

· Over time, this practice helps express emotions clearly and reduces misunderstandings.

Example: During a disagreement, instead of saying, *"You don't care about me,"* Rohan told his wife, *"I feel unimportant when my opinions are dismissed."* This shift in expression led to a more productive conversation.

4. Practicing Gratitude and Positive Affirmations

Objective: Shift focus from negativity to appreciation and self-regulation.

· Start and end the day by listing three things you appreciate about your partner.

· Use affirmations such as *"I am patient and understanding in my relationship."*

· Express gratitude regularly to reinforce positive emotional patterns.

Example: Instead of complaining about household chores, Ananya thanked her husband, Varun, for making her tea every morning. This small gesture improved their daily interactions.

5. Role-Playing Difficult Conversations

Objective: Improve emotional regulation and conflict resolution skills.

· Identify a recurring conflict and role-play different responses.

· Practice expressing concerns calmly and listening actively.

· Reflect on how a mindful approach changes the outcome of the conversation.

Example: Before discussing a sensitive issue about family expectations, Kavita and Arjun practiced their conversation. By role-playing, they learned to avoid accusations and focus on solutions.

6. The Emotional Reset Ritual

Objective: Let go of negative emotions and foster reconnection.

- Create a simple ritual, such as taking a walk, meditating, or listening to calming music, to reset emotions after a disagreement.

- Establish a "reset word" (e.g., *"peace"* or *"reset"*) to signal a fresh start.

- Use this ritual to reinforce a shared commitment to emotional balance.

Example: After arguments, instead of staying upset, Sneha and Rahul started a habit of drinking chai together in silence. This small ritual helped them reconnect and move forward.

Conclusion

Emotional mastery is a skill that requires continuous practice and reflection. By incorporating these exercises into daily life, couples can enhance self-awareness, regulate emotions effectively, and build a more harmonious relationship. Mastering emotions leads to deeper connection, improved communication, and lasting marital happiness.

Key Takeaway from Part 3:

Managing your emotions allows you to approach relationships with patience and understanding, creating a more harmonious and fulfilling connection. However, emotional balance alone isn't enough if unresolved fears and insecurities continue to shape your behavior. Past experiences and deeply rooted beliefs often influence your interactions in ways you may not realize, impacting how you relate to your partner. In the next chapter, we'll explore how these hidden patterns affect your relationships and discuss practical ways to break free from self-defeating habits. True growth begins when you confront and overcome the internal barriers that stand in the way of deeper connection.

Part 4

Overcoming Limiting Beliefs & Self-Sabotage

Chapters:

13. Identifying and challenging negative relationship beliefs
14. Recognizing self-sabotaging behaviors
15. Empathic Accuracy: The Key to a Thriving Marriage
16. Mindset shifts for a healthier love life

Chapter 13

Identifying and Challenging Negative Relationship Beliefs

What we believe about love and marriage affects how we treat our partner and handle challenges. Some beliefs help us grow, while others create problems and misunderstandings. Often, these beliefs come from past experiences, family influences, or society's expectations.

In this chapter, we'll learn how to recognize harmful beliefs, question them, and replace them with healthier thoughts that support a strong and loving marriage.

1. How Beliefs Affect Marriage

Everyone brings certain ideas into a marriage. These beliefs shape how we communicate, handle conflict, and show love.

Some common influences on our relationship beliefs include:

- **Family upbringing:** Watching how our parents or caregivers interacted affects how we view relationships.
- **Past relationships:** If we've been hurt before, we might develop fears or trust issues.

- **Society and culture:** Movies, social media, and traditions can create unrealistic expectations about marriage.
- **Personal insecurities:** How we feel about ourselves affects how we see our partner's actions and words.

When these beliefs go unchecked, they can cause unnecessary stress in a marriage. The key is to become aware of them and make conscious changes.

---

2. Identifying Harmful Relationship Beliefs

To improve your marriage, you first need to recognize beliefs that might be causing problems.

Here are some common negative thoughts people have about relationships:

- *"A good marriage should always be easy."*
- *"If my partner really loves me, they should know what I need without me telling them."*
- *"Marriage means giving up personal happiness."*
- *"If we argue, it means our relationship is failing."*
- *"People never change, so my partner will always act this way."*

To identify your own beliefs, ask yourself:

- What do I expect from my partner and marriage?

- Do I assume my partner should be perfect?
- Have past hurts made me afraid to trust or love fully?
- Are my beliefs helping or hurting my relationship?

Writing your thoughts in a journal can help you see patterns and understand where they come from.

---

3. Replacing Negative Beliefs with Healthy Ones

Once you identify a harmful belief, challenge it by asking:

- Is this belief always true?
- Where did I learn this idea?
- Do I have proof that this belief is correct?
- How is this belief affecting my marriage?

For example, if you believe *"My partner should always know what I need without me saying it,"* ask yourself:

- Is it fair to expect my spouse to read my mind?
- Do I always know exactly what my partner needs without them telling me?
- Wouldn't it be easier to communicate my needs instead of expecting my partner to guess?

Turning Negative Beliefs into Positive Ones

Now, let's replace some common harmful beliefs with healthier ones:

- **Old Belief:** "If we argue, something is wrong with our relationship."

- **New Belief:** "Disagreements are normal. They give us a chance to understand each other better."

- **Old Belief:** "Marriage should be effortless."

- **New Belief:** "A happy marriage takes work, patience, and love from both partners."

By changing the way you think, you can improve the way you respond to challenges in your relationship.

---

4. Practicing Self-Awareness in Your Marriage

Being aware of your thoughts helps you stop negative patterns before they cause problems. Here are some ways to practice self-awareness:

- **Pause and Reflect:** Pay attention to your thoughts about your marriage. Are they based on facts or fears?
- **Talk Openly with Your Partner:** Share your feelings instead of assuming or guessing. Honest conversations build trust.

- **Seek Guidance:** If certain beliefs are hard to change, talking to a counselor or mentor can help.
- **Use Positive Affirmations:** Remind yourself daily that your marriage is built on love, trust, and teamwork.

Conclusion

What you believe about marriage shapes how you experience it. By identifying and changing negative beliefs, you can create a stronger and more loving relationship.

Reflection Exercise:

Write down three beliefs you have about relationships. Are they helping or hurting your marriage? If they are negative, reframe them into positive ones that encourage growth and connection.

By making small changes in how you think, you can build a marriage that is healthier, happier, and more fulfilling.

Chapter 14

Recognizing Self-Sabotaging Behaviors

A happy marriage needs love, trust, and good communication. But sometimes, without realizing it, we do things that hurt our relationship. These actions are called **self-sabotaging behaviors** because they create problems, even when we don't mean to.

Self-sabotage often comes from **fear, insecurity, past experiences, or unrealistic expectations.** If we don't recognize these patterns, they can cause distance, misunderstandings, and frustration in marriage.

In this chapter, we'll talk about common self-sabotaging behaviors, why they happen, and how to stop them. When we understand these patterns, we can take steps to build a stronger, healthier marriage.

---

1. What Is Self-Sabotage in Marriage?

Self-sabotage is when we do things that hurt our relationship, even though we want love and connection. It can happen because of:

- **Past hurts** – If we have been hurt before, we may act in ways to protect ourselves, even when it's not needed.
- **Low self-esteem** – Feeling unworthy of love can make us push our partner away.
- **Fear of closeness** – Some people find it hard to open up emotionally and may avoid deep conversations.
- **Unrealistic expectations** – Expecting a perfect marriage can lead to disappointment.

If we don't recognize these patterns, they can damage our relationship over time.

---

2. Common Self-Sabotaging Behaviors in Marriage

a. Pulling Away from Your Partner

Some people shut down when there's a problem in the relationship. They stop talking or showing affection instead of working through issues together.

Signs of this behavior:

- Ignoring your partner when you're upset.
- Keeping feelings bottled up instead of talking about them.
- Avoiding discussions about problems.

How to fix it:

- Be honest about your feelings. Talk about your emotions instead of shutting down.
- Let your partner know when you need space, but don't stay distant for too long.
- Understand that emotional connection is important in a marriage.

b. Overreacting to Small Issues

Sometimes, small arguments turn into big fights because emotions from the past get mixed in.

Signs of this behavior:

- Getting angry over small mistakes.
- Bringing up old problems during new arguments.
- Thinking the worst about your partner's actions.

How to fix it:

- Pause before reacting. Ask yourself if the issue is really a big deal.
- Focus on solving the problem instead of blaming your partner.
- Let go of past mistakes and move forward.

c. Constantly Seeking Reassurance

Some people feel insecure and need their partner to keep proving their love. While it's normal to want affection, needing constant reassurance can create pressure in a relationship.

Signs of this behavior:

- Asking your partner if they love you all the time.
- Feeling anxious when your partner is busy or not paying attention.
- Worrying that your partner will leave you, even without a reason.

How to fix it:

- Build confidence in yourself and your relationship.
- Trust your partner's love based on their actions, not just words.
- Enjoy the relationship instead of constantly looking for proof of love.

d. Keeping Score

Marriage is not about keeping track of who does more. But some people count every effort and expect their partner to do the same.

Signs of this behavior:

- Feeling upset when your partner doesn't match your efforts exactly.
- Bringing up past favors or sacrifices.

- Expecting something in return for every good deed.

How to fix it:

- Focus on teamwork instead of competition.
- Give love freely without expecting something back every time.
- Appreciate what your partner does instead of counting what they don't do.

e. Avoiding Difficult Conversations

Some people avoid talking about problems because they fear conflict. But avoiding issues only makes them bigger over time.

Signs of this behavior:

- Changing the subject when your partner talks about concerns.
- Pretending everything is fine instead of discussing problems.
- Hoping issues will disappear on their own.

How to fix it:

- Be open to discussing difficult topics calmly.
- Focus on finding solutions instead of avoiding the conversation.
- Remember that talking about issues strengthens your relationship.

3. How to Stop Self-Sabotaging Behaviors

a. Be More Self-Aware

Pay attention to how you act in your relationship. Ask yourself:

- Am I acting based on past fears or the present situation?
- How do my actions affect my partner?
- What can I do differently to improve my marriage?

b. Communicate Honestly and Kindly

Good communication prevents misunderstandings. Instead of assuming your partner knows what you need, share your feelings clearly and calmly.

c. Challenge Negative Thoughts

If negative thoughts appear, ask yourself:

- Is this thought true, or is it based on fear?
- Is there evidence to support this belief?
- Can I look at this situation in a more positive way?

For example, if you think *"My partner doesn't care about me,"* ask yourself:

- What actions has my partner taken to show love?
- Could I be misinterpreting their behavior?
- How can I express my needs instead of assuming the worst?

d. Be Kind to Yourself

Nobody is perfect. Instead of blaming yourself for past mistakes, focus on learning and improving. Treat yourself with kindness and patience.

e. Get Help If Needed

If self-sabotaging behaviors are hard to change, talking to a therapist or relationship coach can help. There is no shame in seeking guidance to improve your marriage.

Conclusion

Self-sabotage can create problems in marriage, but it doesn't have to. By recognizing these behaviors and making small changes, you can create a relationship built on love, trust, and understanding.

Reflection Exercise:

1. Identify one self-sabotaging behavior you notice in yourself.
2. Write down how it affects your marriage.
3. Think of one step you can take to change it.

Small changes can make a big difference. Start today!

Chapter 15

Empathic Accuracy: The Key to a Thriving Marriage

Understanding Empathic Accuracy

Empathy is the ability to understand and share the feelings of another person. More specifically, empathic accuracy refers to the skill of accurately identifying and interpreting the thoughts and emotions of others. This ability strengthens interpersonal relationships by allowing individuals to respond in ways that foster understanding and emotional support.

In many cases, people do not explicitly express their true emotions. Their words may not fully reflect their inner thoughts or feelings. For example, a wife may verbally express confidence about a divorce but exhibit signs of distress through her body language and tears. Such discrepancies highlight the importance of empathic accuracy in discerning underlying emotions beyond spoken words.

The Role of Empathic Accuracy in Marriage

Empathic accuracy is particularly crucial in marital relationships, where emotional attunement influences satisfaction and longevity. Couples who can accurately gauge each other's feelings tend to build stronger bonds, whereas those who struggle with this skill may face miscommunication and conflict.

Why It Matters

· **Enhanced Communication:** Identifying unspoken emotions allows partners to address concerns before they escalate.

· **Effective Conflict Resolution:** Understanding a partner’s perspective fosters patience and empathy in resolving disagreements.

· **Strengthened Emotional Connection:** Feeling understood and valued deepens trust and intimacy.

For instance, if a husband notices his wife appearing withdrawn after a social gathering, he can gently ask about her feelings instead of assuming disinterest or irritation. Such moments of attentiveness reinforce emotional closeness and mutual support.

Personality Traits and Empathic Accuracy

Personality traits influence how individuals interpret emotions and interact with their partners. Understanding these traits enhances empathic accuracy by offering insights into predictable patterns of behavior.

How Personality Traits Play a Role

· **Predicting Behavior:** Traits such as openness, conscientiousness, and agreeableness shape emotional responses and coping mechanisms.

· **Improving Social Awareness:** Recognizing personality-driven tendencies helps partners anticipate each other's needs and reactions.

For example, a highly conscientious husband who values structure and predictability may struggle with last-minute changes. His spontaneous wife, who enjoys flexibility, may inadvertently frustrate him by altering plans without notice. Recognizing this, she can communicate changes in advance to ease tension and maintain harmony.

Empathic Accuracy and Attachment Styles

Attachment behaviors, often shaped by early life experiences influence how individuals express and perceive emotions in relationships.

Key Connections between Personality and Attachment

· **Anxious Attachment:** Individuals with higher neuroticism may seek frequent reassurance yet hesitate to vocalize their needs due to fear of rejection.

· **Avoidant Attachment:** Those who prefer emotional distance may struggle with verbalizing feelings, leading to misunderstandings.

Building emotional rapport is essential in navigating these attachment behaviors. Marriage counselors and mediators invest time in developing trust to accurately assess individuals' emotional states and interpersonal dynamics.

A Personal Example

A woman once shared how her husband's avoidant attachment style initially caused distress in their marriage. His silence during arguments felt like emotional withdrawal, making her feel ignored and undervalued. Over time, she learned that his quietness was his way of processing emotions rather than a sign of indifference. Understanding this allowed her to approach conflicts with greater patience and reassurance, ultimately strengthening their bond.

Empathy in Action: The Three Dimensions of Love

Marriage is built upon three fundamental expressions of love:

1. **Attachment:** The emotional bond that fosters security and connection.

2. **Caregiving:** The instinct to nurture and support one another.

3. **Desire:** The physical and romantic aspect of the relationship.

Given the complexity of marriage, developing empathic accuracy is essential for maintaining harmony. Partners who actively listen, observe nonverbal cues, and understand each other's emotional needs are better equipped to sustain a fulfilling relationship.

Strategies for Strengthening Empathic Accuracy in Marriage

Practical Steps:

· **Learn Your Partner's Personality Traits:** Understanding stable behavioral tendencies helps in predicting reactions.

· **Observe Nonverbal Cues:** Facial expressions, tone, and gestures often reveal unspoken emotions.

· **Foster Emotional Intimacy:** Create an open environment where both partners feel safe to express themselves.

· **Study Attachment Styles:** Recognizing attachment-related behaviors aids in addressing emotional needs effectively.

Empathy as an Ongoing Practice

Empathic accuracy is not a fixed trait but a skill that evolves over time. Life changes, personal growth, and shifting dynamics require continuous adaptation. Regularly refining this ability helps couples remain emotionally attuned and resilient in their relationship.

Real-Life Application

Consider a couple adjusting to parenthood. With increased responsibilities and stress, emotional expressions may become less clear. By prioritizing empathy, they can ensure they remain connected, supporting each other through the transition instead of allowing misunderstandings to create distance.

By mastering empathic accuracy, couples can build deeper emotional connections, navigate challenges with greater ease, and create a marriage founded on mutual understanding and trust. This skill not only enhances romantic relationships but also enriches all meaningful human connections.

Chapter 16

Mindset Shifts for a Healthier Love Life

The way we think about love and marriage shapes our relationship. If we believe love should always be effortless, we may get frustrated when challenges arise. If we think our partner should "just know" what we need, we may feel disappointed when they don't.

Shifting the way we think can transform our marriage. Instead of reacting out of frustration, we start responding with patience, understanding, and love. Instead of feeling stuck, we see opportunities to grow together.

Let's explore key mindset shifts that will help you nurture a healthy, lasting relationship.

---

1. Shift from "Me vs. You" to "We Are a Team"

Anecdote:

Emma and Jake used to argue over household chores. Emma felt Jake wasn't doing enough. Jake felt Emma was always nagging. Every conversation turned into a battle—until they changed their mindset. Instead of blaming each other, they started asking, "How can we handle this as a team?" They divided tasks in a way that felt fair, and the fights stopped.

New way of thinking:

Instead of *"I need to win this argument,"* try *"How can we solve this problem together?"*

How to apply this shift:

- Remind yourself that you're partners, not competitors.
- When disagreements arise, focus on solutions instead of pointing fingers.
- Celebrate each other's strengths and support each other's weaknesses.

---

2. Shift from "Love Should Be Easy" to "Love Takes Effort"

Example:

Imagine you plant a garden. If you don't water it, the plants wither. Marriage is the same. It thrives when you nurture it with love, patience, and effort.

New way of thinking:

Instead of *"If we truly love each other, things should just work out,"* think *"A strong marriage is built with care and commitment."*

How to apply this shift:

- Make time for meaningful conversations, even during busy days.
- Show love in small ways—leave a sweet note, send a kind text, give a hug.
- Accept that challenges are normal and use them to grow together.

---

3. Shift from "My Partner Should Make Me Happy" to "Happiness Starts with Me"

Anecdote:

Liam expected his wife, Sarah, to always cheer him up when he was stressed. When she didn't, he felt unloved. Over time, he realized he was putting too much pressure on her. He started taking care of his own happiness—going for walks, listening to music, and pursuing hobbies. As a result, their relationship improved.

New way of thinking:

Instead of *"My partner should always make me feel happy,"* shift to *"I am responsible for my own joy."*

How to apply this shift:

- Find personal activities that make you happy.

- Appreciate your partner's support but don't expect them to fix your emotions.
- Bring your best self into the relationship instead of waiting for happiness to come from outside.

---

4. Shift from "My Partner Should Read My Mind" to "I Need to Communicate Clearly"

Example:

Mia was upset when her husband forgot their anniversary. She thought, *"He should know how much this means to me."* But he wasn't a mind-reader. The next year, she told him a month in advance, "I'd love to do something special for our anniversary." This time, he planned a surprise dinner.

New way of thinking:

Instead of *"If they love me, they should just know what I need,"* try *"I will express my needs clearly."*

How to apply this shift:

- Speak up about your feelings instead of expecting your partner to guess.
- Use "I" statements: "I feel loved when you…" instead of "You never…"
- Encourage open conversations where both partners feel heard.

---

5. Shift from "Marriage Should Be 50/50" to "Marriage Requires 100% from Both of Us"

Anecdote:

David and Lisa used to keep score. If Lisa cooked, she expected David to do the dishes. If David planned a date, Lisa felt she owed him something in return. Over time, they realized a great marriage isn't about keeping things even—it's about giving wholeheartedly.

New way of thinking:

Instead of *"I'll only put in effort if my partner does,"* think *"I will give my best to this marriage."*

How to apply this shift:

- Do kind things for your partner without expecting something in return.
- Be patient when your spouse is struggling—they'll do the same for you later.
- Remember that love is about giving, not calculating.

---

6. Shift from "Conflict Means We Have a Problem" to "Conflict Helps Us Grow"

Example:

Imagine two people speaking different languages. Without effort, they won't understand each other. Marriage is similar—disagreements are chances to learn each other's language.

New way of thinking:

Instead of *"We should never fight,"* shift to *"Healthy conflict can bring us closer."*

How to apply this shift:

- Stay calm during disagreements—focus on understanding, not winning.
- Listen carefully before responding.
- Look for solutions instead of dwelling on problems.

---

7. Shift from "I Need to Fix My Partner" to "I Accept My Partner as They Are"

Anecdote:

Samantha always tried to change her husband, Mike. She wanted him to be more outgoing, more romantic, more like the guy in her favorite movie. The more she pushed, the more distant he became. When she finally accepted him for who he was, their marriage became more peaceful and loving.

New way of thinking:

Instead of *"My partner needs to change for me to be happy,"* think *"I appreciate my partner for who they are."*

How to apply this shift:

- Focus on your partner's strengths instead of their flaws.
- Support their personal growth, but don't try to control them.
- Remember, love is about acceptance, not perfection.

---

8. Shift from "Love Should Always Feel Exciting" to "Love Grows in Different Ways"

Example:

Think of a bonfire—it starts with bright flames but eventually settles into warm, steady embers. Love works the same way. It may not always feel exciting, but it deepens into something even more meaningful.

New way of thinking:

Instead of *"We should always feel the same passion as when we first met,"* shift to *"Love matures and becomes deeper over time."*

How to apply this shift:

- Embrace new ways of showing love, like deep conversations and shared goals.
- Find new adventures together, even in small ways (like trying a new restaurant).
- Appreciate the comfort and security of long-term love.

Conclusion

Your thoughts shape your relationship. By shifting your mindset, you can strengthen your marriage and build a deeper, healthier love.

Reflection Exercise:

1. Which mindset shift do you struggle with the most?
2. How has your current way of thinking affected your marriage?
3. What small change can you make today to shift your mindset?

A great marriage doesn't happen by accident—it's built with love, understanding, and the right mindset. Start making these shifts today!

Key Takeaways from Part 4:

Letting go of self-imposed barriers paves the way for personal growth and transformation. However, overcoming negative beliefs is only the first step. Lasting change happens when we replace doubt with self-compassion, creating space for confidence to grow. The next phase of this journey involves recognizing our worth, building a positive self-image, and developing the assurance needed for meaningful relationships. In the next chapter, we'll explore how to nurture self-love and confidence, empowering ourselves to live with authenticity and purpose.

Part 5

Building Self-Love & Confidence

Chapters:

17. How Self-worth Influences Relationship Success
18. Practices for self-care and self-validation
19. Guided journaling for personal growth

Chapter 17

How Self-Worth Influences Relationship Success

Have you ever felt unappreciated in your relationship? Do you sometimes question whether you are "good enough" for your partner? Or do you often seek validation in your marriage?

These feelings stem from self-worth—the way we perceive and value ourselves. A strong sense of self-worth helps build healthy, fulfilling relationships, whereas low self-worth can lead to insecurity, resentment, and emotional distance.

In this chapter, we'll explore how self-worth affects relationships and how to cultivate a healthier self-image that strengthens your marriage.

---

1. Understanding Self-Worth

Self-worth is the internal belief that we are valuable and deserving of love and respect, independent of others' opinions.

Example:

Imagine two individuals applying for the same job. One walks in confidently, knowing their skills and contributions are valuable. The other is hesitant, doubting their own worth. Who is more likely to succeed?

Similarly, in marriage, if you believe you are worthy of love, you will attract and maintain a healthier relationship. However, if you doubt your worth, you may struggle with trust, communication, and emotional intimacy.

---

2. How Low Self-Worth Affects Relationships

When we struggle with self-worth, it often manifests in our relationships. Here's how:

1. Seeking Constant Reassurance

If you feel unworthy, you may frequently seek validation from your partner. While occasional reassurance is natural, excessive dependence on external affirmation can be draining for your spouse.

Example:

Ananya constantly asks her husband, "Do you really love me?" multiple times a day. Despite his reassurances, she continues to doubt his feelings, making him feel frustrated and unheard.

Mindset Shift: Work on building confidence from within rather than expecting your partner to fill the void.

2. Fear of Abandonment

People with low self-worth may irrationally fear that their partner will leave them, leading to jealousy, possessiveness, or emotional withdrawal.

Example:

Rohan always worries that his wife will find someone "better." He frequently checks her phone, questions her friendships, and constantly seeks reassurance. His insecurity, rather than bringing them closer, creates tension in their marriage.

Mindset Shift: Trust is the foundation of love. If you feel insecure, reflect on whether this stems from past wounds or your own self-doubt.

3. Accepting Less Than You Deserve

When people don't value themselves, they may tolerate mistreatment—such as disrespect, neglect, or even abuse—because they feel unworthy of better treatment.

Example:

Priya remains in a marriage where her husband rarely acknowledges her emotions. She convinces herself, "Maybe I am just being too sensitive," instead of recognizing that she deserves to be heard and respected.

Mindset Shift: You deserve kindness and respect. The way you allow others to treat you often reflects how you see yourself.

3. How Healthy Self-Worth Leads to Relationship Success

When you cultivate a strong sense of self-worth, your relationship naturally flourishes. Here's why:

1. You Bring Your Best Self to the Relationship

Feeling secure in yourself allows you to contribute positively to your marriage. You become more patient, loving, and emotionally balanced.

Example:

Vikram embraces his strengths and doesn't seek constant validation from his wife. As a result, he loves freely without fear or insecurity, making their relationship stronger.

2. You Set Healthy Boundaries

People with high self-worth express their needs and set clear boundaries. They don't tolerate disrespect or neglect.

Example:

Neha tells her husband, "I love you, but open communication is important to me. We need to discuss our issues instead of avoiding them." She values herself enough to advocate for a healthy dialogue.

3. You Build a Secure and Loving Connection

When you feel secure in yourself, you don't project unnecessary fears into your relationship. This creates a peaceful, trusting bond.

Example:

Arjun trusts his wife and doesn't feel the need to check her messages or seek constant validation. His confidence in himself strengthens their marriage.

---

4. Building Self-Worth for a Stronger Marriage

If you struggle with self-worth, it can be improved. Here's how:

1. Practice Self-Compassion

Be kind to yourself. Instead of criticizing your flaws, treat yourself with the same compassion you would offer a friend.

Example:

Instead of saying, "I always mess things up," try, "I am constantly learning and improving."

2. Recognize Your Strengths

Take time to acknowledge your unique qualities. What makes you a good partner?

Exercise:

Write down five things you love about yourself and remind yourself of them daily.

3. Avoid Comparisons

Your marriage is your journey. Comparing yourself to others can make you feel inadequate.

Example:

Instead of thinking, "They have a perfect marriage, and we don't," remind yourself, "Every relationship has challenges, and we are working on ours in our own way."

4. Prioritize Self-Care

Your mental, emotional, and physical well-being matter. Taking care of yourself enhances your confidence and energy in your relationship.

Try this:

- Exercise regularly
- Pursue hobbies you enjoy
- Surround yourself with supportive people
- Practice gratitude daily

5. The Power of Self-Worth in Love

When you embrace your worth, your relationship transforms. You stop settling for less, communicate openly, and build a deeper connection with your partner.

Final Thought:

A healthy marriage starts with a healthy YOU. The more you value yourself, the more love, respect, and joy you invite into your relationship.

Reflection Exercise:

1. Do you rely on your partner for validation?
2. Do you set healthy boundaries in your relationship?
3. What is one step you can take today to improve your self-worth?

Your marriage is only as strong as your relationship with yourself. When you cultivate self-love, your relationship will flourish!

Chapter 18:

Practices for Self-Care and Self-Validation

A healthy marriage begins with a healthy you. When you prioritize self-care and self-validation, you bring a stronger, more balanced version of yourself into your relationship. This chapter explores simple yet effective ways to nurture yourself emotionally, mentally, and physically so that your marriage can thrive.

1. The Foundation of Self-Care

Before you can nurture your relationship, you must take care of yourself. Self-care is not selfish; it is essential. It allows you to show up fully for your spouse without feeling drained or resentful. Think of it like refilling your cup so you can pour into your relationship without running empty.

Practical Self-Care Habits:

- **Emotional Care:** Expressing your feelings through journaling, talking to a trusted friend, or seeking professional guidance when needed.

- **Mental Well-being:** Practicing mindfulness, setting boundaries, and taking breaks from stressful situations.

· **Physical Health:** Maintaining a balanced diet, getting enough sleep, and engaging in physical activity to boost your energy and mood.

Example: Priya, a mother of two, always prioritized her family's needs over her own. Over time, she felt exhausted and irritable. When she started setting aside 30 minutes a day for a morning walk and quiet reflection, she noticed a shift—she was calmer, more patient, and able to connect with her spouse in a more meaningful way.

2. The Power of Self-Validation

Many people seek validation from their spouse to feel valued and loved. While appreciation in a relationship is important, relying solely on external validation can create insecurity and frustration. Self-validation means recognizing your worth and acknowledging your feelings without needing constant reassurance from others.

Steps to Self-Validation:

· **Acknowledge Your Feelings:** Instead of dismissing emotions, accept them as real and valid.

· **Practice Positive Self-Talk:** Replace negative self-judgment with kind and affirming words.

· **Celebrate Small Wins:** Take pride in your daily efforts, even if no one else notices.

· **Trust Your Decisions:** Avoid second-guessing yourself based on others' opinions.

Example: Ravi always doubted his decisions, constantly seeking approval from his wife. This led to unnecessary conflicts. Once he started affirming his choices and trusting his instincts, he felt more confident, and their relationship became more harmonious.

3. Setting Boundaries for a Balanced Life

Healthy boundaries protect your time, energy, and emotional well-being. Without them, you may feel overwhelmed or taken for granted. Setting clear boundaries helps you maintain self-respect while fostering a more respectful and understanding marriage.

Ways to Set Healthy Boundaries:

· **Communicate Needs Clearly:** Let your spouse know what you need to feel supported.

· **Learn to Say No:** Protect your personal time and energy without guilt.

· **Prioritize Alone Time:** Having personal space allows you to recharge and show up as your best self.

Example: Meera felt pressured to always be available for her husband, even when she needed time to unwind. Once she openly communicated her need for some quiet time after work, her husband understood, and their interactions became more positive.

Self-Care and Relationship Growth

When both partners invest in their well-being, the marriage naturally flourishes. Prioritizing self-care and self-validation helps reduce resentment, improves communication, and strengthens emotional connection.

Ways to Integrate Self-Care into Marriage:

· **Support Each Other's Growth:** Encourage your spouse's personal development and self-care practices.

· **Share Your Self-Care Routines:** Exercise together, meditate, or engage in hobbies that bring you joy.

· **Check-In Regularly:** Discuss what's working and what needs improvement in maintaining balance.

Example: Arjun and Kavita introduced a weekly 'self-care check-in,' where they shared their personal well-being goals. This not only kept them accountable but also deepened their emotional connection.

Final Thoughts

Your marriage will be at its best when you take care of yourself first. Prioritizing self-care and self-validation isn't just a personal benefit—it's an investment in the health and happiness of your relationship. When you feel good about yourself, you bring out the best in your marriage.

Chapter 19

Guided Journaling for Personal Growth

Journaling is a simple yet powerful way to understand yourself better. It helps you reflect on your thoughts, emotions, and actions, making it easier to build a strong and healthy marriage. By writing down your experiences, you can see patterns in your behavior, improve communication, and deepen your connection with your spouse.

1. Why Journaling Helps in Marriage

Marriage requires understanding and patience. Writing in a journal allows you to express your feelings, recognize areas for improvement, and strengthen your relationship. It helps you manage emotions and communicate better.

Example: Meera often felt ignored by her husband but didn't know how to express her emotions. When she started writing about her feelings, she realized she had been holding back. This helped her speak openly with her husband, Rohan, leading to better understanding.

2. How to Start Journaling

You don't need special skills to start journaling. Just grab a notebook and write whatever is on your mind. Follow these simple steps:

- **Make it a habit:** Set aside a few minutes daily or weekly.
- **Write honestly:** Express your thoughts freely.
- **Use prompts:** Guided questions can help you stay focused.
- **Look back:** Reviewing past entries can show how much you've grown.

Example: Arjun, a busy professional, started journaling for five minutes before bed. Over time, he became more relaxed and attentive in conversations with his wife, Nisha.

3. Journaling Prompts to Help You Grow

Here are some simple questions to guide your journaling:

Self-Reflection Prompts:

- What do I like about myself?
- How do I handle stress, and how can I improve?
- How have my past experiences shaped how I communicate with my spouse?

Relationship Prompts:

- What do I appreciate about my spouse?

- How do we express love differently?
- What are some common disagreements, and how can we handle them better?

Emotional Growth Prompts:

- What emotions did I feel today, and why?
- How can I be more patient and kind in my marriage?
- What personal boundaries do I need for a healthier relationship?

Example: Priya, who often felt overwhelmed with work and home, answered the question, "What boundaries do I need?" She realized she needed to share household responsibilities and talk to her husband, Karan, about it. This improved their teamwork.

4. Journaling to Improve Communication

One major cause of misunderstandings in marriage is poor communication. Journaling helps by:

- Allowing you to process feelings before reacting.
- Helping you organize thoughts before discussing them.
- Identifying unresolved issues that need attention.

Example: Raj used to withdraw after arguments, making Anjali feel distant. Writing down his thoughts helped him understand his fear of conflict. Over time, he learned to talk things through instead of shutting down.

5. Journaling Together as a Couple

While personal journaling is valuable, sharing the experience with your spouse can bring you closer. You can try:

- **Couple's journaling:** Writing about goals, dreams, or challenges together.
- **Letter writing:** Writing letters to each other and exchanging them.
- **Gratitude journaling:** Writing down things you appreciate about each other.

Example: Deepak and Sanya started writing one thing they loved about each other daily. This simple habit made them feel more appreciated and connected.

Final Thoughts

Journaling is a great way to grow as a person and strengthen your marriage. It helps you understand yourself, express emotions, and communicate better. Start today, and see how small reflections can lead to big changes in your relationship.

www.ingramcontent.com/pod-product-compliance
Ingram Content Group UK Ltd.
Pitfield, Milton Keynes, MK11 3LW, UK
UKHW021407190726
13845UKWH00028B/938

9 788192 496917